Alastair Weir.

SHIONA AIRLIE

&

BRIAN J. R. BLENCH

EDITED BY
CHRISTINE HUDSON

Front cover photos:

Top from left: *Sir George Hay; Dumbarton glassworks, 1815; wine glass engraved by John Millar; sculpture by John Airlie, engraved by Norman Orr*

Bottom: *19th century glassmaker* Courtesy Glass Study Association, France

Rear cover photos:

Top row, from left: *Advertising paperweight from John Baird; Clutha jug designed by Christopher Dresser*

Bottom row, from left: *Monart trumpet vase; detail of Paul Ysart paperweight*

Scotland's Glass: 400 Years of Glassmaking, 1610–2010

Edited by Christine Hudson

Foreword by Frank Andrews

Proofread by Christine Hudson, Brian Blench, Frank Andrews, Denis Hebden and David P. Encill

Additional images courtesy of Frank Andrews, www.scotlandsglass.co.uk, and Denis Hebden

Photography at Edinburgh, Glasgow and Bennie museums by David P. Encill

Image editing by David P Encill

Book design by David P Encill

First published in the UK in 2009 by Cortex Design
Birmingham, UK
www.cortex-design.co.uk

Printed and bound in the UK by The Print Network (UK) Ltd
www.theprintnetwork.co.uk

Typeset in 10pt Myriad Pro

ISBN-10: 0-9549196-5-3

ISBN-13: 978-0-9549196-5-8

Contents

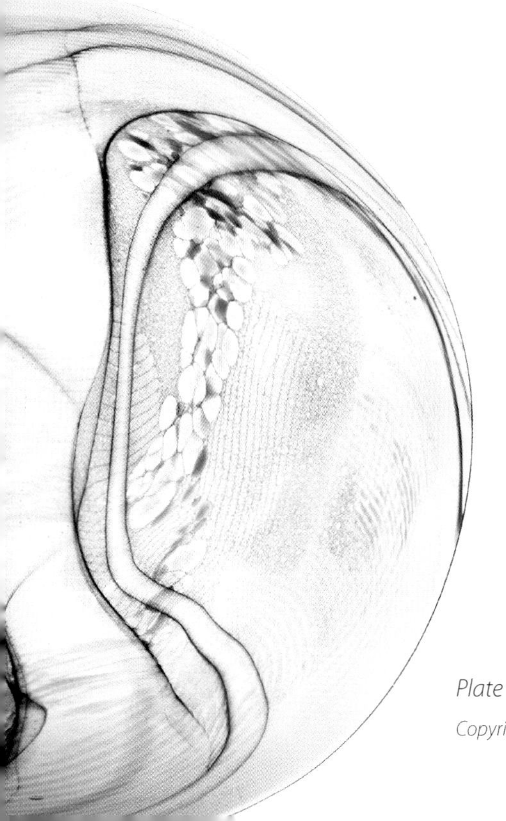

Plate by Fleur Tookey

The Authors

Shiona Airlie

Shiona Airlie studied history of art at Edinburgh University and then took a postgraduate diploma in art gallery and museum studies at the University of Manchester. She worked as exhibitions officer in Edinburgh Museums before moving to Glasgow to set up the touring exhibition programme there.

The daughter of a glassmaker, her final post in Glasgow was as the curator of the Dutch and the glass collections. Shiona left that post to become the first director of the National Glass Centre in Sunderland, where she remained until 1998. She now maintains her interest in glass by contributing to scotlandsglass.com, and has volunteered her expertise to assist in the 400th anniversary celebrations.

Shiona also writes on Sino-British history and has published two books and numerous papers on the subject, as well as many biographical dictionary entries. A third biography has recently been commissioned from her.

Bibliography

Reginald Johnston Chinese Mandarin: Chinese Mandarin, 2000

Thistle and Bamboo: The Life and Times of Sir James Stewart Lockhart, 1990

Brian J. R. Blench

Brian Blench studied at the universities of Cambridge, Copenhagen and London. After teaching for a while, he entered the museum profession as education officer at the Worcestershire County Museum at Hartlebury Castle, Hartlebury, where he first became involved with the glass industry. In 1973, Brian was appointed keeper of decorative art, specialising in glass and costume, at Glasgow Museums and Art Galleries.

In 1979, Brian was the founder chairman of the Scottish Glass Society. He was the chairman of the International Council of Museums Committee for Museums and Collections of Glass from 1983 to 1989. He took early retirement in 1992, and was a consultant to Christie's fine and decorative arts course at the University of Glasgow, before moving to Argyll.

Bibliography

Brian has written many articles on diverse subjects since 1962. The following are a few related to glass.

The Art of Glass, catalogue of an exhibition on the work of Helen Monro Turner and John Lawrie, 1972

Contemporary Scottish Glass, exhibition catalogue, Glasgow Museum and Art Galleries, 1979

Venetian Glass, Glasgow Museums and Art Galleries, 1982

Alison Geissler – Glass Engraver, exhibition catalogue, Glasgow Museums and Art Galleries, 1983

"Scottish Glass: 1945 to Present Day," *Journal of Glass Studies,* **25,** 1983

"Christopher Dresser and His Glass Designs," Annales du 9eme Congrès de l'Association Internationale pour l'Histoire du Verre, Leige, 1985

"Helen Monro Turner and the Revival of Scottish Glassmaking," *The Glass Cone,* **17,** Spring 1988

James Couper, Alexander Jenkinson, John Moncrieff. articles in *Scottish Dictionary of Business Biography,* **II,** 1990

"From Coffee Machines to Clutha Glass: Notes on Couper's City Glassworks", *Scottish Art Review,* **XVII,** 1991

Foreword

by Frank Andrews

Glassmaking is often seen as a mundane industry, but, when explored in depth, it provides a fascinating insight into the social and economic history of a nation as well as the richness of its art. Scotland has featured on the world stage in many areas of industry and the arts, but its 400-year-old glass industry is an almost ignored part of its rich heritage.

Scotland possessed the basic raw materials: superb sand; the coal much needed for an energy-intensive product; and, above all, the people with the vision to exploit and produce glass.

Throughout these 400 years, Scotland has been happy to import the knowledge, skills and ideas required and then to develop them to great effect. Italians, Bohemians, Spanish, Germans and Americans have all come to Scotland and added their magic to the industry. One woman, Helen Monro Turner, even founded a glass education heritage that has produced some of the finest artists and craftspeople.

The country has been a world leader in glass for use in steam engines, seen the renaissance of paperweight making and of the paperweight as an art form, and produced some phenomenal stained glass, art glass and glass engraving. Throughout, the country's economy has challenged glassmakers' ingenuity but, although the industry is seemingly in decline, the number and the quality of the glass artists show no signs of diminishing.

As a collecting area, glass caters to a huge variety of interests and pockets, and is one of the few areas where those still working in Scotland today can make affordable arts and crafts to your exact requirements.

Frank Andrews

Co-author, *Ysart Glass*
www.ysartglass.com
www.scotlandsglass.co.uk
www.glass-study.org

A message from Alison Geissler

As 400 years is only four of my lifetimes (I am currently 102), I have been invited to write a few words for this fascinating book, which covers all aspects of Scottish glass – one of my great interests.

When collecting wartime ration cards at the Edinburgh College of Art, I was encouraged to return to try glass engraving, and immediately felt at home. This set me on a fascinating career, with the excitement of bringing flat glass to life, that lasted over 50 years. From this, grew my interest in all aspects of glass. I shall therefore treasure this wonderful vista of glass history.

Alison Geissler, MBE

Suggested reading

Devine, T.M., *The Scottish Nation, A History,* 1700–2000, Viking, 1999

Donnelly, Michael, *Scotland's Stained Glass – Making the Colours Sing*, The Stationery Office, Edinburgh, 1997

Hall, Robert G., *Scottish Paperweights,* Schiffer Publishing, 1999

Mahoney, Colin, *Masterworks: The Paperweights of Paul Ysart,* Paperweight Press, 2009

Selman, Lawrence H., *The Art of the Paperweight: Perthshire,* Paperweight Press, 1983

Simmonds, John, *Paperweights from Great Britain 1930–2000,* Schiffer Publishing, 1999

Smout, T.C., *A History of the Scottish People: 1560–1830,* Collins, 1970

Smout, T.C., *A Century of the Scottish People: 1830–1950,* Collins, 1986

Terris, Colin, *The Charlton Standard Catalogue of Caithness Paperweights*, Charlton Press, 1999

Turnbull, Jill, *The Scottish Glass Industry 1610–1750,* Monograph Series No. 18, Society of Antiquaries of Scotland, 2001 (The author is currently working on a sequel covering the period 1750 to 2006.)

Turner, Ian, Clarke, Alison J. and Andrews, Frank (with introduction by Brian Blench), *Ysart Glass,* Volo Edition, 1990

Woodward, H. W., *The Story of Edinburgh Crystal,* Dema Glass Ltd, 1984

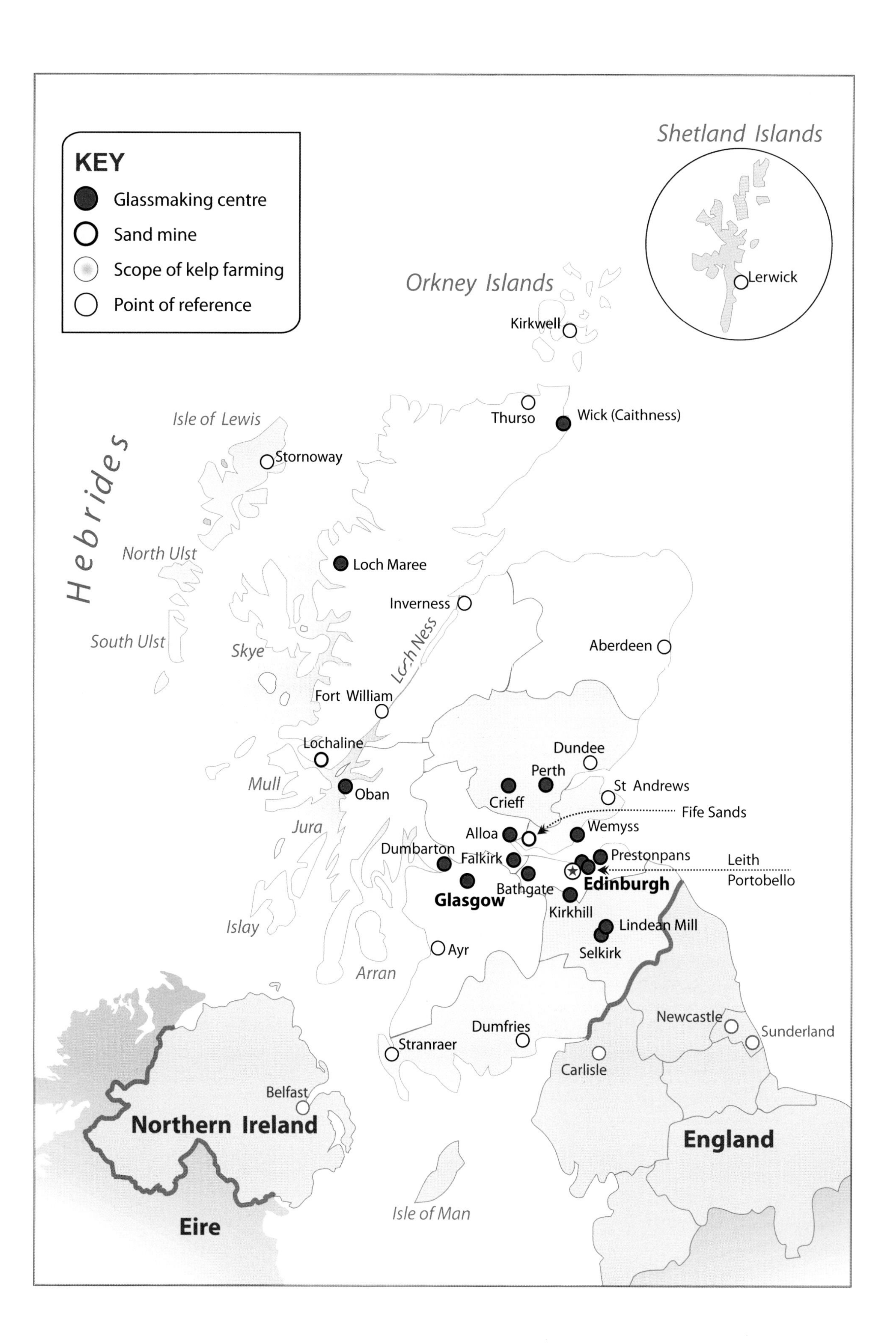
KEY
Glassmaking centre
Sand mine
Scope of kelp farming
Point of reference
Shetland Islands
Lerwick
Orkney Islands
Kirkwell
Thurso
Wick (Caithness)
Isle of Lewis
Stornoway
Hebrides
North Ulst
Loch Maree
Inverness
South Ulst
Skye
Loch Ness
Aberdeen
Fort William
Lochaline
Dundee
Perth
Mull
Oban
Crieff
St Andrews
Fife Sands
Jura
Alloa
Wemyss
Dumbarton
Falkirk
Prestonpans
Leith
Portobello
Edinburgh
Glasgow
Bathgate
Kirkhill
Islay
Lindean Mill
Selkirk
Ayr
Arran
Newcastle
Sunderland
Dumfries
Stranraer
Carlisle
Belfast
Northern Ireland
England
Eire
Isle of Man

Chapter 1
The 17th Century

When James VI of Scotland inherited the English throne in 1603, he made an unseemly dash for London. He left his native country behind with hardly a backward glance, for Scotland had little to charm its monarch. A poor country covered with rough tracks and overwhelmingly inhabited by peasants, it held few attractions for the sophisticated or learned man. Towns were small, and, in the case of Edinburgh, cramped and stinking. Most people worked the land at subsistence level, and only a few Scots lived in any sort of style. It was hardly the kind of place one would choose to establish a business aimed at the luxury market, and yet, in 1610, that was exactly what George Hay of Nethercliff did when he sought and was granted by the king the first patent to make glass in Scotland.

Nowadays a world without glass is unthinkable, but for centuries that was the reality for most Scots. When Hay was granted his patent, glass was a luxury item imported from England or the Continent and was only found in the grandest of houses. The wealthiest landowners still lived in fortified homes with tiny, frequently glassless, window openings and used pewter, wood or pottery to adorn their dining tables. Only the richest owned drinking glasses, and then probably only one or two. For example, an inventory of Kilmarnock Castle (now known as Dean Castle) in 1611 shows that his Lordship owned not a single glass. All the drinking vessels were pewter, and all the light fittings were made of metal.

A stone carving of Sir George Hay, part of the Kinnoull memorial, at the Kinnoull Aisle, near Perth.

Smailholm Tower near Kelso, Roxburghshire, has its origins in the 15th century and is a typical Scottish tower house with tiny window openings.

Copyright © Jim MacRae

In this environment, Hay was taking a big gamble in seeking to set up a glass industry of any sort in Scotland. He must have known that the market for his wares was going to be limited to say the least, but he had sufficient vision (or blind optimism) to believe that he could make his glassworks a success. Scotland might have been an impoverished nation in 1610, but the economy under James VI was stable and growing, and Hay, as an entrepreneur with many commercial interests, saw an opportunity and seized it.

Hay's earliest output would almost certainly have been window glass. Churches, of course, had used glass to great effect in their windows for centuries, but the use of glass in houses was a relatively recent introduction; parchment and oiled linen were the most common window coverings. Window glass was expensive, and until the 1560s, when Flemish glassmakers began producing crown glass in England (the kind that produces a "bullseye"), all window glass had to be imported. To have large windows installed in one's property was a statement of wealth used to great advantage by several English nobles in the later 16th century, but the fashion had not yet spread to Scotland.

Hay moved in the most elevated of social circles. A man who knew how to wield influence and make money, he became James VI's Lord High Chancellor and was later a Privy Councillor for Charles I in Scotland. He would have been aware of the innovations in England and Europe, and obviously thought it worth his while to introduce the new fashion for glass windows into his native country.

Burghley House, Lincolnshire. The north front, completed in 1587, is a fine example of the new fashion for glass windows, though only the richest English nobles could afford them.

Copyright © Burghley House

The glass industry came late to Scotland, despite the country having an abundance of the three essential resources for making glass: fuel, in the form of wood and later coal; fine silica sand; and kelp as a source of soda ash to help the sand to melt at a lower temperature. Hay needed to set up his glass furnace in an area with these close at hand. Until recently, it was believed that he established his first glassworks at Wemyss Bay in Fife. However, Jill Turnbull in her invaluable book *The Scottish Glass Industry 1610–1750* makes a strong case that the first furnaces were actually sited at Loch Maree in Wester Ross.

The remoteness of the site would have been no bar to making glass. This was a time when most roads in Scotland were so bad that they were impassable for wheeled vehicles of any sort, so water transport was preferential for moving goods over large distances. Loch Maree had plenty of wood to fire the furnaces, which is why Hay had an ironworks there, and fine sand to make the glass. If the first Scottish glass furnace was at Loch Maree, nothing survives today and it appears to have been a short-lived concern lasting at best, Turnbull estimates, until the mid-1620s. Hay may also have established, or had an interest in, a glassworks at Wemyss Bay where the locally known "Glass Cave" can still be seen on the foreshore.

It was typical of the founder of the Scottish glass industry that he quickly looked to expand his production, but to do this he had to find men capable of making high-quality glassware such as drinking vessels. Glassmakers were skilled workers who were paid a great deal more than the average labourer, but they kept their trade secrets closely guarded.

A disc of crown glass being spun. The disc could reach up to one-and-a-half metres in diameter.

From Mirror for Chance, 1951

A bullseye. Crown glass was made by gathering a large ball of molten glass, blowing it into a globe, opening out the globe and then spinning it to make a large disc. The centre point, to which the spinning rod was attached, gave the bullseye. The finished circle of glass then had to be cut carefully to get the maximum number of small panes of glass from it, as this cutting diagram laid over the bullseye shows..

Copyright © Science Museum/Science & Society picture Library, www.scienceandsociety.co.uk

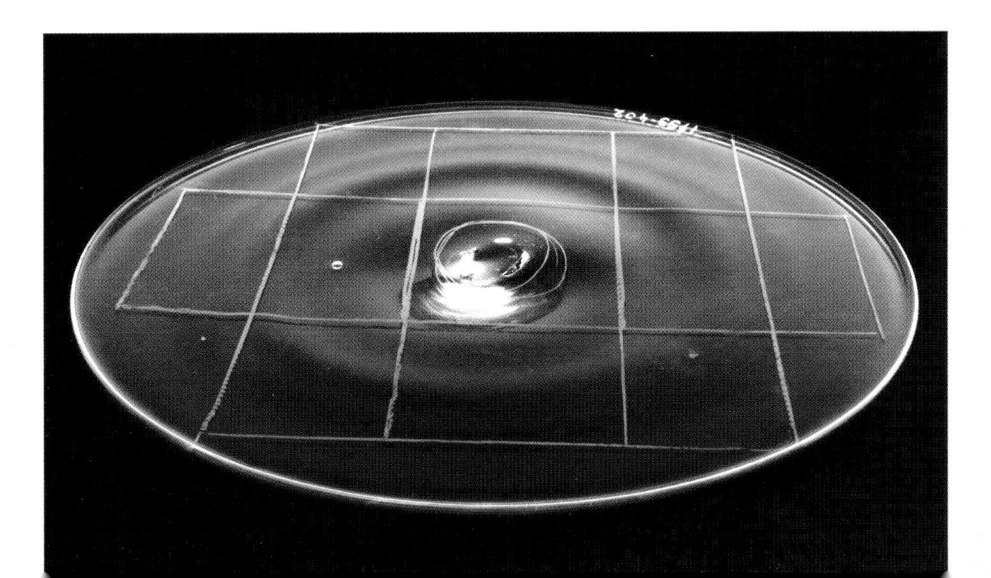

It was migrant Italians who excelled at making vessels of the highest quality that began fine glassmaking in England in the late 16th century. Venice had long been a centre of glassmaking, and the city state jealously guarded her glassmaking secrets for centuries by confining her master craftsmen to the island of Murano. However, some makers managed to escape and over the years moved west, first to the Netherlands and then to England. Hay had no compunction about enticing these men even further north, much to the annoyance of the English manufacturers who had paid good money to bring skilled workers and their families from mainland Europe. So many Venetians moved into Scotland during this period that the Venetian Ambassador in London noted that most of his compatriots brought to work in London had moved north by 1622.

A Venetian glass tankard made in the late 16th century. This intricate and very beautiful piece of glass shows the mastery of the Venetian glassmakers and the skills they brought to the rest of Europe. When it was made, only the wealthiest of patrons could afford such a fragile luxury.

Copyright © Culture & Sport Glasgow (Museums), Spitzer collection

Turnbull credits Hay with establishing a glass operation that flourished for several years. Employing Italian glassworkers meant that he could expand his range of wares, and by the 1620s his furnaces were making not only window glass but also glass bottles and drinking glasses. Although the windows and bottles were made solely for the Scottish market, he produced sufficient drinking glasses to be able to export them, again to the annoyance of English glassmakers. Such was his success, that in 1620 English makers petitioned the king to ban the import of glass into England, except when shortages occurred, in which case, Scottish glass could be imported.

Sadly, one can scour the museums of the world and not find a single example of Hay's production. If any of his glass survives, it is now attributed to an anonymous maker. What we do know about Hay's production is that it would have been typical of the early 17th century: bottles with high, kicked bases for stability and elegant wine and ale glasses with deep bowls, plain stems and large bases. Only the finest homes would have boasted a Hay glass, but there is always the hope that, one day, a glass that can be firmly attributed to one of his factories will surface from a dusty castle cupboard.

A 17th century bottle with a kicked base. Although this is probably English, Hay's glassmakers would have made similar items. The seal is very indistinct, but the date shown is 1688 and it was possibly made for the Globe Inn.

Courtesy Broadfield House Glass Museum

In the early 1620s, Hay seems to have been in partnership with James Ord, a glass vessel manufacturer who employed Venetian glassmakers at Morison's Haven, near Prestonpans in East Lothian. Business partnerships were common at that time, and businessmen frequently moved in and out of these relationships with ease. A joint venture was a good way of spreading the risk in any enterprise, and it may be that Hay found Prestonpans a better site for reaching the wealthy market in Edinburgh and its environs than remote Loch Maree.

Morison's Haven was a good site with plentiful coal nearby and potteries in the area to produce the melting pots. Hay and Ord's works made thousands of drinking glasses each year, and large numbers were exported to England, despite the export ban. Morison's Haven was a flourishing, if short-lived, concern producing bottles, vessels and windows. Mirrors may also have been produced, as Paul Le Blanc is known to have made wooden mirror frames at his workshop in nearby Prestongrange.

The situation changed suddenly in 1627 when Sir Robert Mansell, who already held the patent for glassmaking in England, bought out Hay's monopoly and closed down the furnaces that had produced the cheaper, green glass normally used for bottles or everyday vessels. Hay (though not his family) disappeared from the glass industry at this point. Created a peer by Charles I in 1627 and then Earl of Kinnoull in 1633, he died in 1634. His memorial in a small chapel in Kinnoull in Perthshire should be a place of pilgrimage for everyone interested in Scottish glass.

Mansell eventually appears to have closed down the works at Morison's Haven, though Italian glassmakers somehow managed to continue operating there until the 1640s, and an English traveller saw glass being made on the shore at Prestonpans in 1661.

Although the first phase of glassmaking in Scotland lasted but 30 years, its demise was not, in all probability, due to a lack of customers. Hay was probably justified in his belief that a market for glassware of all types could be created in Scotland. Estate papers from merchants show that by the 1640s drinking glasses were being used by not only the upper classes but also merchants and small landowners. The markets for window glass and bottles also grew enormously in the same period.

Hay's memorial, Kinnoull Aisle, Perthshire.

A mid-19th century coloured engraving by W.E. Bartlett of Leith pier and harbour.

This was an age when everyone drank ale in preference to the insanitary drinking water and celebrated with the odd whisky. The landed and upper classes were developing a taste for wine, so the need for glass bottles was growing steadily. Probably, the first flourishes of a glass industry folded owing to unrest across the country. The Covenanters fired their voice of protest in 1638, and marched into England two years later. A decade after that, Cromwell invaded Scotland. Looting and civil unrest are not good bedfellows for any emerging industry, which would explain the lack of new glass furnaces in Scotland until after the restoration of Charles II in 1660.

The next glass factory about which anything is known was established by Robert Pape in 1663 in the Leith Citadel, a fort that had been built on Cromwell's instructions in 1656 and almost completely demolished by Charles II just five years later to leave only a portion bounded by Leith Links. The City of Edinburgh was, at the time, one of the most crowded in the country, and there was no room in the old town for a glass factory of any sort; thus Leith, the port of Edinburgh, was as close as a glassmaker could get to the capital. Leith was to remain a centre of glassmaking for the next 200 years.

Pape's factory, the Citadel Glasshouse, was not a thriving business. He had difficulty in selling his glass, either because the quality was not good enough or because it was overpriced, and so he sold his patent to make glass in 1665. However, the glass factory did not prosper under its new management either. Pape, a Scot, employed Edward Dagnia, an Italian, as his master glassmaker. Dagnia, who had already worked at Prestonpans, was contracted to make wine bottles, beer glasses and fine wine glasses. Although Dagnia died within two years of starting work for Pape, his sons continued at the Citadel Glasshouse.

Despite the contracts, the glasshouse appears to have produced mainly bottles and only small quantities of drinking glasses: primarily beer glasses rather than fine wine goblets. However, the works marks the start of a truly commercial industry in Scotland. Leith was ideally situated for glass manufacture. It was a perfect base from which to trade with the multitude of ships sailing to and from the port. It was also a wine trading centre, and the raw materials to make glass were easily brought into the harbour.

A firing glass. These glasses were designed with thick bases so that they could be banged on a table to celebrate a toast. Although this is probably an 18th century example, this type of glass was made as early as the 17th century in Scotland.

Prestonfield House in Edinburgh. Designed by Sir William Bruce in 1687, it is exactly the kind of new, grand house that the North Leith makers would have provided glass for.

Reproduced with acknowledgement to Peter Stubbs, www.edinphoto.org.uk

Despite Pape's failure, it was not long before another businessman set up a glasshouse in Leith. Opened in North Leith in 1673 by Sir James Standsfield, within five years it was such a success that Standsfield employed a team of glassmakers and was trying to recruit others from Newcastle upon Tyne, which had become a centre of fine glass of all types. That he had to recruit so many glassmakers from England suggests that the tradition of keeping the secrets of making glass in the family continued throughout the 17th century.

Standsfield's works made bottles, phials, window glass and drinking vessels. The works probably also made specialist glasses such as firing glasses with thick bases so that they could be banged on the table after toasts, along with bowls, brandy glasses, hour glasses, tumblers and dishes. The glassworks closed in 1682, possibly as the result of a disagreement between the partners, and the contents of the factory were sold at auction in an effort to cover their losses and pay debtors, including the workmen they had employed.

It appears that Standsfield was undeterred by this setback, as he bought the business back at auction with a new partner and installed a manager and glassblowers from Newcastle upon Tyne to restart the North Leith Glassworks. The closure and reopening

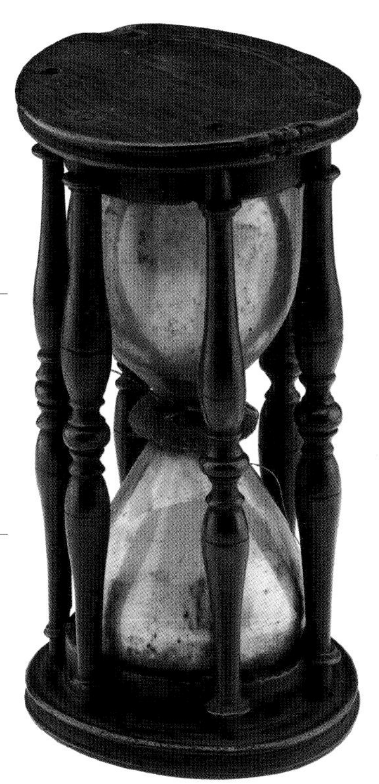

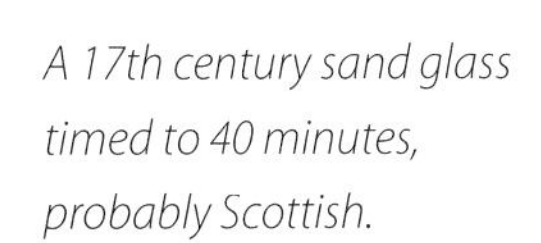

A 17th century sand glass timed to 40 minutes, probably Scottish.

Courtesy National Museums of Scotland

of the glasshouse in North Leith came at a time of a great development in glassmaking – the process of producing lead crystal. This was first made in England, and it was not long before Scottish makers also discovered that by adding lead oxide to the batch they could achieve glass that was clearer and more brilliant than before. Better still, it was ideal for engraving and cutting, thus offering new decorative possibilities.

Standsfield was not slow to adopt this innovation, and his revitalised works began producing the new, brilliant flint glass, as it had become known, along with bottle and window glass. His glass team was contracted to make 1,200 wine or beer glasses every week of production, and may also have made glass handles for swords or knives. Green glass bottles and phials, and apothecaries' containers were also made on the site.

According to contemporary sources, North Leith glass was of a quality comparable with the best glass produced in England, but Standsfield and his partners never managed to make their works a real commercial success. Although the bottle making was profitable, Standsfield had to petition the Scottish government, just as Pape had done 20 years earlier, for protection against foreign, and particularly English, imports.

Standsfield was murdered in the winter of 1687, and a new company took over his works a few months later. In an effort to make the business profitable, it concentrated on making bottles and apothecaries' wares, but still struggled. The works were reportedly in a most rundown state, but continued to make bottles and containers throughout the 1690s, a period of tremendous economic uncertainty. Even so, by 1696, Leith was employing 122 glassblowers in its glasshouses.

In 90 years, glassmaking in Scotland had developed into an industry that could produce high-quality wares, but it was still a risky business and few factories lasted any length of time. However, the glassmakers had reason to be optimistic as the century neared its close. By the 1680s, tastes were changing in country houses, and Sir William Bruce was designing his first grand mansions for Scottish clients, complete with large windows. These new houses boasted dining rooms that required fine glassware, from goblets to mirrors and chandeliers. It must have appeared a good time to invest in a glass business that could produce quality glass of any sort.

A 17th century stirrup cup made in the Venetian style. This one is said to have been used by James VI at Dunfermline in 1603 to sup a farewell drink before he left Scotland for London.

Copyright © National Museums of Scotland

Mirror making was one such glass specialism that flourished in this economy. It was a dangerous business that used highly toxic chemicals, including mercury, so mirror makers required great skills. One Edinburgh maker, James Turner, boasted in 1678 that no one else could make mirrors of a similar quality anywhere in the land, even though he depended on imported plate glass to make his wares. However, by the 1690s, plate glass was being made in Scotland, and Turner had sufficient trade to employ more than one mirror maker, including Hugh McGhie who was based in Edinburgh's Canongate.

Just as it appeared that Scottish glassmakers would benefit from new techniques and an expanding market, a series of devastating famines throughout the 1690s hit the country. Even the prosperous port of Leith was not immune to the effects and people died of starvation on its streets. Only with the union of the parliaments in 1707, which opened up the English and overseas markets to Scottish makers, did the industry expand again.

Chapter 2
The 18th Century

The 18th century in Scotland is usually associated with the Enlightenment and the building of Edinburgh's glorious New Town. Indeed, it was a period of rapid economic growth, and the glass industry benefited from the country's improving prosperity, both around Edinburgh (mainly in Leith) and in Glasgow and the west of Scotland. But it should not be forgotten that during this period Scotland also experienced two Jacobite rebellions and the union of its parliament with that in England: events that were to have direct, if different, impacts on Scottish glass.

It was a time when Scottish cities changed enormously. Edinburgh expanded outward from the stinking squalor of the old town, and Glasgow developed from a pretty little town into a great commercial centre. This growth in the west was due partly to the burgeoning linen and tobacco trades, and the merchants and landowners who were increasingly willing to spend their wealth on grand houses with fine fitments. At the beginning of the century, one glass factory in Edinburgh and another in Glasgow provided almost all the glass Scotland required. However, the demand for glass grew to such an extent that, by 1795, 14 glass factories existed across the country. They employed more than 1,000 people who received relatively high wages in return for their skills. Eight of the factories produced bottles, four made crown glass for windows and the other two specialised in wares of all types in lead glass.

A pair of goblets with a matching carafe made in the second half of the 18th century. The glassmaker has used the brilliance of lead glass to great effect in cutting the stems and bowls, and has added touches of engraving around the tops of the glasses. The facet-cut stems would have glistened beautifully in a candlelit drawing room.
Courtesy Lauriston Castle Trust

The Citadel Glasshouse became known as the Edinburgh and Leith Glass Company in the early 18th century. Various owners came and went, and output waxed and waned accordingly, and may even have ceased for a period in the 1730s. At the beginning of the century, it was supplying good-quality wine and ale glasses to fashionable households throughout Scotland. Receipts for its wares survive in various archives. However, the company achieved its greatest fame by blowing two of the largest bottles ever made in Britain. In 1747, a bottle of 94-gallon capacity was made. Four years later, the glassmakers excelled with an even larger bottle holding an astonishing 105 gallons. It was blown by the principal director of the glassworks, Thomas Summers.

Despite these record-breaking bottles, the company fell into financial difficulties and was bought and restarted by a group of brewers. By the end of the century, it was being run successfully with Archibald Geddes as its manager under the name of the Edinburgh Company's Glasshouse. The company gradually diversified, and by the early 19th century it was making a variety of glasswares in plain and coloured glass.

A mirror made between 1770 and 1780 with its original glass.

In 1747, the partners of the glasshouse in North Leith expanded the business and built another glasshouse, this time in South Leith. Many of the partners were involved in the wine and spirit trade, and so the glasshouse concentrated on making bottles. As a result, with a market for its wares virtually guaranteed by its owners, the business flourished. It is telling that the South Leith glasshouse was a success simply because of the business interests of many of its owners. The union of the parliaments in 1707 had provided both incentives and problems for Scottish glassmakers. On the one hand, it put them in direct competition with the far larger industry in England, and they also lost the protection the Scottish government had given them against imports. On the other hand, it opened up a vast new market that many Scottish entrepreneurs sought to exploit. At the close of the century, the Leith bottle house was still producing large quantities of bottles under the able management of Duncan Gavine. Gavine and Geddes were to remain important members of Leith's glassmaking community well into the following century.

A toastmaster's deceptive glass made about 1720. Gentlemen's clubs became increasingly popular in the 18th century, and many appointed a toastmaster to propose all the toasts. To ensure he stayed sober throughout the proceedings, special glasses like this were used. It looks like an ordinary glass, but has a tiny bowl that holds just enough for the toastmaster to empty at each toast and not become drunk.

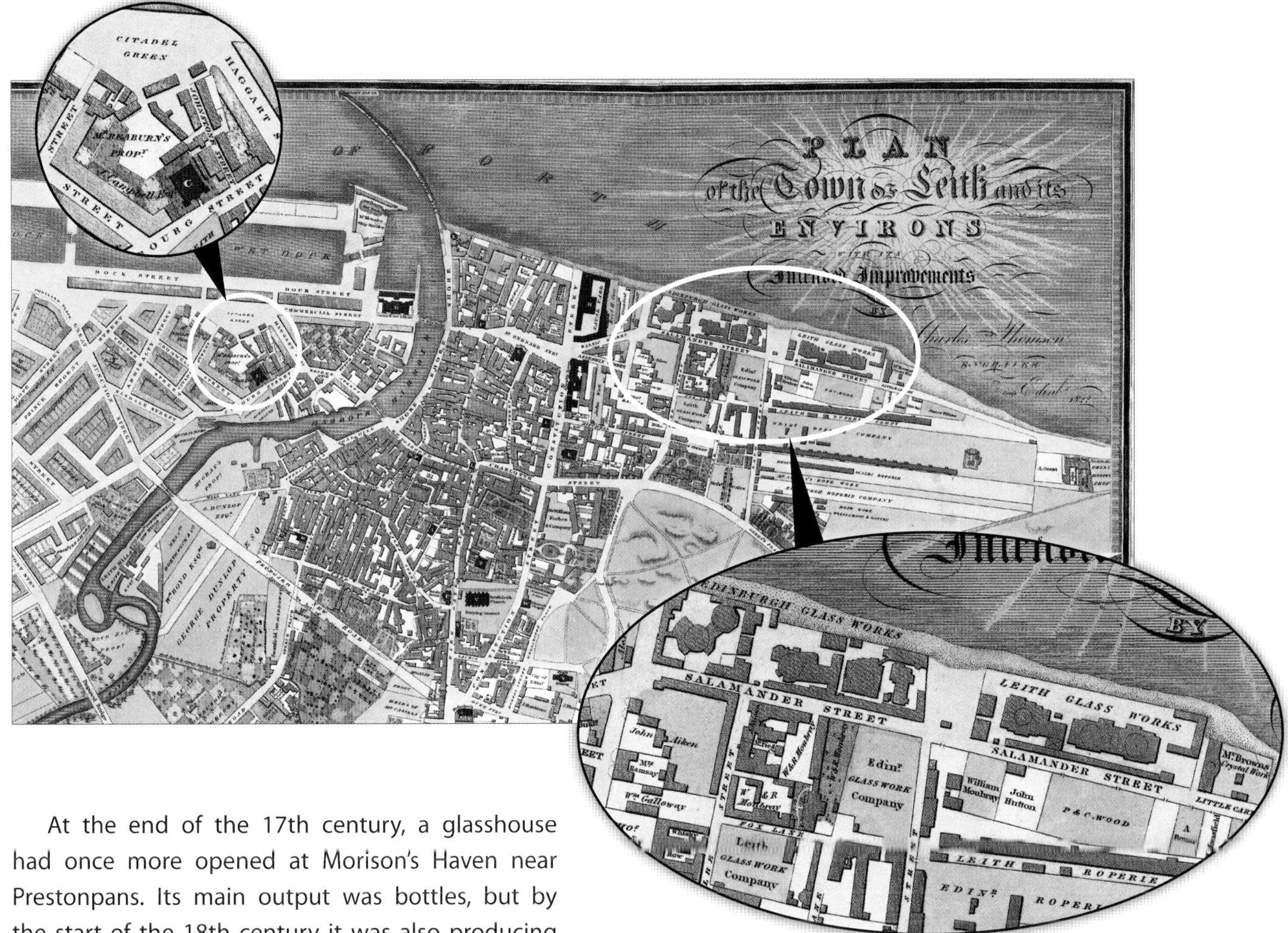

At the end of the 17th century, a glasshouse had once more opened at Morison's Haven near Prestonpans. Its main output was bottles, but by the start of the 18th century it was also producing plate glass for mirrors and coach and domestic windows. At least some of the output seems to have gone to North Leith, where, towards the end of the 17th century, William Scott set up a company that specialised in mirrors and coach glass. A flourishing business employing more than 20 people, it initially had to import plate glass from England. But within a short time of the Morison's Haven works opening, Scott appears to have been persuaded to use the Scottish product.

A map of Leith dated 1822 showing the Edinburgh and the Leith glassworks. The Citadel Green (top left) was originally named "City-Dale".

A rare set of teardrop glasses from Castle Semple in Renfrewshire. Made in the early 18th century, these resemble the glasses being produced in factories such as Morison's Haven. Clients frequently purchased sets of glasses from the factory, but few have survived.

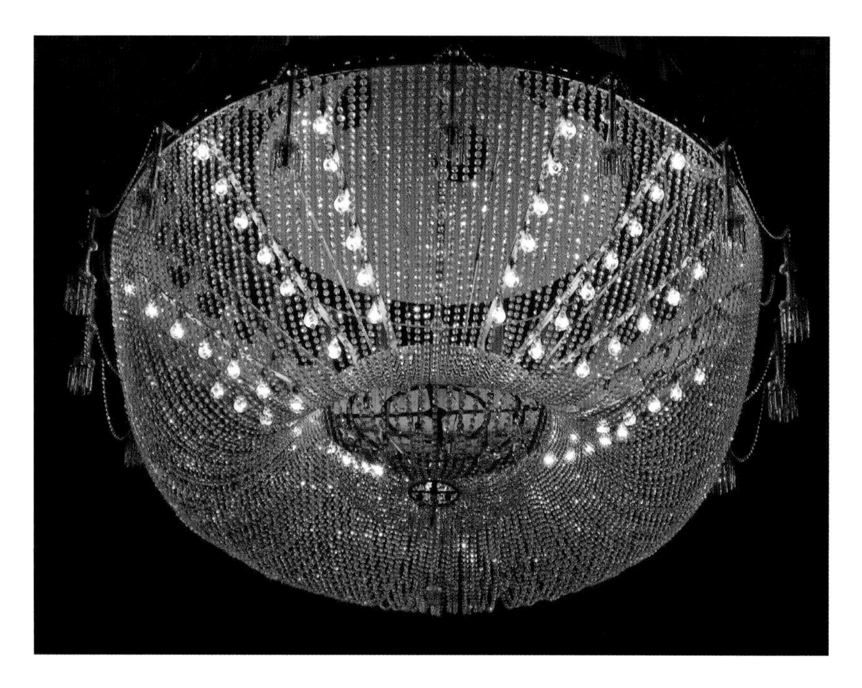

The Edinburgh Assembly Rooms chandeliers. These were remodelled by the Ranken family in 1834 so that they could be lit by gas. The cost of more than £450 for this work included almost £300 for additional glass drops.

Two large goblets, 30-cm tall, made and engraved in Edinburgh between 1780 and 1782. They were a present from the city to the then Lord Provost, the Honourable David Stewart. One is decorated with the Edinburgh coat of arms.

Although the Morison's Haven works was initially successful (there are records that show gentry in East Lothian buying several sets of glasses from Morison's Haven), it struggled to find a market for its flint glass in the longer term and the bottles it made faced stiff competition from the works in Leith. Despite producing what appears to have been high-quality glass, the works at Morison's Haven closed in 1727, probably owing to the financial mismanagement of its owner, William Morison. Once more, Scottish mirror and coach glassmakers were forced to look to the English market for their glass. Fortunately, glass was easily procured from the south, as the union of the parliaments had removed import restrictions.

The Geddes family became one of the most influential forces in the world of Scottish glass in the 19th century, but they were not alone. The Rankens, who also began working in glass in the 18th century, were to become equally important in their area of expertise in the following century. James Ranken set up a glass factory in the middle of Leith Walk in 1773. A lapidary by training, he used his cutting skills to produce luxury items such as brilliantly cut girandoles and chandeliers.

The Broomielaw, Glasgow, in 1819. In this drawing, the glass cone of the bottle factory can clearly be seen.

Before too long, he had a rival manufacturer of such items in Verreville of Glasgow. In 1798, the company was taken over by Francis Ranken, who continued to produce a similar range of items. Francis was patronised by the best and wealthiest of Scottish nobility, and his greatest memorial can still be seen: the magnificent chandeliers he produced for the Assembly Rooms in Edinburgh's George Street. The Ranken family owned the company until the 1840s.

Glasgow got its first glasshouse at the beginning of the 18th century. Founded by James Montgomery and partners, it was sited near the Broomielaw Quay. When Montgomery initially petitioned parliament to open a bottle factory, his application was, unsurprisingly, opposed by Morison of the Morison's Haven works. However, Montgomery's arguments in favour of building a bottle factory in the west of Scotland were persuasive. The road system between Edinburgh and Glasgow was, at the time, incredibly poor and unsuitable for wheeled vehicles. This gave the merchants of Glasgow the options of transporting in their bottles via a long sea journey or on horseback across the central belt; both were hardly viable propositions, given the bulky and fragile nature of the goods.

Montgomery was granted his permit, and by 1702 the company was producing a variety of bottles. Even after Montgomery died in 1733, the company continued successfully, and in 1742 the glassworks expanded into a new site on Jamaica Street, beside the first glasshouse. Despite changes of ownership, the bottle making business flourished and in 1752 it also began to make window glass. It was the first of many such factories to emerge in the west of the country. The Glasgow bottle works was the first truly successful Scottish glasshouse. Long-lived and highly productive, it provided containers for local merchants and vintners. Squat, heavy and durable, thousands of bottles made their way around the globe filled with ale, wine or spirits.

Left: A wine bottle from the Glasgow works impressed with the seal 1765 Walter Maclae. It became fashionable in the 18th century to have bottles personalised, as they were a cheaper alternative to the far more expensive lead glass decanters.

Far left: A green bottle probably made in the Glasgow bottle works and bearing the seal Kilmarnock 1713. One of the earliest examples of a Scottish bottle to survive, it may have been made for Lord Kilmarnock.

The glass made in Scottish factories is often difficult to identify, as much of it so closely resembles English and Irish glass as to be indistinguishable. English and Irish glassmakers frequently worked in Scottish factories, particularly after 1707, and brought their techniques with them. What is certain is that by the 18th century a lot of very high-quality glass was being made in Scotland and that, even today, a considerable amount of it is mislabelled as English. It is clear from contemporary records that Scottish clients bought considerable quantities of glass from local factories in preference to importing it from England.

The next glasshouse to be built in Scotland was founded in Alloa, Clackmannanshire, by Lady Frances Erskine in 1750. Lady Frances, one of the rare female entrepreneurs of the time, hoped to bolster the family's dwindling finances with this venture. Much of the Erskine wealth had been built on the Fife coalfields, but the price of coal slumped following the Jacobite uprising in 1745. Lady Frances's father, the Earl of Mar, had encountered glassmakers in Bohemia during his travels in Europe. Knowledge of the Bohemian makers allied with a desire to improve the economy of the area spurred Lady Frances into opening a bottle factory. She invited Bohemian glassmakers and their families to Alloa to supervise the building of the works and to train native Scots in the art of glassmaking.

A pair of glasses with air-twist stems that belonged to the owners of Craigrothie Castle. Made in the middle of the 18th century, this type of glass was the height of fashion. The air-twist effect is achieved by pricking the molten glass to form air bubbles. The stem is then drawn out, which stretches the bubbles, and twisted to make a delicate pattern.

Bottle making was closely linked to the wine trade, much of which was through the port of Leith. But the Seven Years' War, which started in 1756, cut off wine supplies from France, and further trouble in America and Europe effectively closed the European wine market to Britain for most of the 1770s and 1780s. This obviously had an impact on the market for Alloa bottles, and Lady Frances sold the business in 1767 to a consortium of businessmen who were mainly ale bottlers and wine merchants. They ensured that, despite the lack of foreign wine, the Alloa works flourished. It was ideally situated across the Forth from Leith and so could easily access the Edinburgh market. Whisky was an increasingly favoured alternative to the scarce foreign wine, and ale was drunk by almost everybody. Taverns and whisky stills flourished. In Edinburgh alone, then a city of 75,000 people, it is estimated that in 1778 there were over 400 stills and more than 2,000 taverns, and they all needed bottles.

The ties between Alloa and the capital city were strengthened even more when Thomas Elder and Archibald Geddes, partners in the Edinburgh Glass Works in Leith, bought the Alloa works in 1788. This was an important year for the industry, as Britain made peace with France, and an agreement to lower wine tariffs was reached. The bottle industry expected to expand, and it made sense for the Edinburgh men to take over the bottle works in Alloa rather than see it become a direct competitor to their works in Leith.

As was typical of 18th century businesses, the partnerships constantly changed, but the Alloa company flourished under all its various owners. By the end of the century, it had grown from a one-and-a-half acre site to cover four acres. Despite the disruption of the Napoleonic Wars (c. 1799–1815), it was still a flourishing concern at the beginning of the 19th century.

Glasgow in the 1770s was a pretty little town with, as one visitor said in 1772, "delightful orchards and picturesque buildings," but it lacked a top-quality glassworks. This changed around 1776 when the Verreville works was founded by Dr Patrick Colquhoun on a three-acre plot on the banks of the Clyde at Finnieston. The site was well situated for the supply of the essential coal and sand, and from the outset, Colquhoun intended to produce glass of the highest quality, as good as anything made on the Continent.

If anyone could achieve this standard, it was Colquhoun. Born in Dumbarton in 1745, Colquhoun became one of the city's business power brokers when he moved to Glasgow. Lord Provost of the city three times, he established the Glasgow Chamber of Commerce, the first of its kind in Britain, in 1783. Such an energetic businessman naturally had no time to oversee the making of Verreville glass, so he wisely brought a talented group of glassmakers from Tyneside to run the company. The glass they made was destined for the upper end of the market; of the clearest quality, it was turned into fine decanters, candlesticks, bell pulls, chandeliers and the like. Highly decorative, the expensive Verreville pieces were affordable by relatively few Scots, and, from the beginning, much of it was exported.

A late 18th century decanter engraved JME and decorated with swags, sun symbols and a goat. The decoration could be an adaptation of the Incorporation of Skinners' coat of arms, but in the late 18th century symbols were often used as decoration and to amuse the learned gentleman. In this instance, the sun probably represents the sun god Apollo and symbolises art, invention and inspiration, whereas the goat represents Bacchus the god of drink and wild living. Each time the owner, JME, looked at this decanter, he would be reminded that although drinking could inspire great thoughts, it could equally lead to debauchery.

A pair of cut-glass candlesticks made in the18th century.

Verreville expanded swiftly, using the port of Glasgow with great efficiency to send its wares to the new colonies that had been established in America. In the 1780s, the glassmakers who Colquhoun had brought in to build the Verreville brand bought the business from him. This new company included two partners from the thriving English glass town of Newcastle upon Tyne, Charles Williams and Isaac Cookson, and a solitary Glaswegian, merchant Alexander Ritchie. Colquhoun was no fool. The American War of Independence, which ended in 1783, had effectively closed the American market to the glass business. How he managed to persuade his glassmakers to buy the business at such an unfortunate time is a mystery, but buy it they did. All too quickly, their dreams evaporated and Verreville was ruined. Banker and merchant Gilbert Hamilton bought them out with the intention of improving the business by exporting wares to the Far East and the West Indies. But even Hamilton struggled, and in 1795 he employed a glassmaker called John Geddes, who we will encounter in the next chapter, to run the works.

In 1776, the Dumbarton Glass Company was established to make high-quality glass in the west of the country. At the time, Dumbarton was the closest port on the Clyde to Glasgow that was navigable by large ships. Founded by the Dixon family, Dumbarton Glass Company quickly became a large factory that also produced chemicals. More than 300 people worked there by the end of the century. The works built a reputation for making the finest crown glass for windows as well as bottles of all types, but it was perhaps best known for the wheel engraving that decorated the glasses. Much of this engraving was done in the factory, but the company also used outworkers to cope with the demand for its engraved glass.

By the end of the century, the glass market was a far larger one than that which had existed 100 years earlier. Ownership of glass was no longer the preserve of the wealthy, although it remained a relatively expensive commodity. The great building programmes in both Edinburgh and Glasgow provided ready markets for window glass. Lamps, candlesticks and even chandeliers were in great demand by the rising middle classes.

A Dumbarton bottle richly decorated with crimping, painted decoration and gilding, including the words W C Real Mountain Dew and portraits of Tam o' Shanter and Souter Johnnie, both figures from Burns' poem, Tam o' Shanter. Dumbarton was just one of the factories that were quick to use the popularity of Robert Burns as inspiration for their wares.

The Dumbarton works in 1815.

A large square bottle made at Dumbarton.

An 18th century dram glass of a type typically used to drink whisky from. What makes this one special is that it was the poet Robert Burns' own dram glass.

Ladies now drank claret, previously the preserve of men, and preferred to do so from elegant wine glasses. Whisky was becoming a favourite drink, and toddy lifters were a peculiarly Scottish by-product. Even ale, once supped from wooden or pottery cups, was increasingly drunk from a glass. This was also the century in which champagne first appeared and fuelled the need for yet another type of drinking glass. There appeared to be no end to the variety of glasses that factories now had to produce.

Some of the most beautiful glasses from the 18th century are known as Jacobite glasses. Many of these have apparently innocent decoration on them, such as flowers, that secretly symbolised support for the House of Stuart. After his defeat in 1746, Prince Charles Edward fled Scotland, but within a few years he had become a rather fanciful and romantic figure to many, and his memory and the Jacobite cause were celebrated by some fine, and now highly prized, glasses.

Scottish glass factories also made more everyday objects. Some, such as sandglasses, had a useful purpose. Common in churches, they were essentially giant egg timers made to last for up to an hour before the sand had all run from one end to the other, and were used to ensure ministers did not overrun their allotted sermon times. Window glass for houses continued to be an important part of the trade, and the increasing demand for coach travel also provided work.

The first coach service from Edinburgh to Glasgow began in 1749, though it was an uncomfortable and none-too-profitable affair. Putting glass windows in coaches was one way to improve the service, and in July 1754, the Edinburgh Stage Coach proudly advertised in the *Edinburgh Courant* that it had fitted glass windows for the comfort of its passengers.

A toddy lifter. The hot drink made from whisky and called toddy was popular in the 18th and 19th centuries. The lifter has a hole at both ends. To serve the toddy, one plunged the lifter into a bowl of toddy and put a finger over the narrow neck end. When the lifter was raised out of the liquid, releasing the finger let the toddy flow into a glass. Lifters were a fairly standard size and gave a single measure of the drink.

A wine glass with an opaque twist stem that is reputed to have been used by Prince Charles Edward when he was in Stirling at the beginning of 1746. These stems are made in a similar way to air twists, but using canes of white or coloured glass instead of air bubbles.

An 18th century sedan chair that, like the coach, required thicker plate glass in its windows to minimise cracking through movement. Sedan chairs were frequent sights on the narrow streets of Edinburgh's Old Town, which, in the 18th century, still had streets and closes too narrow for carriages.

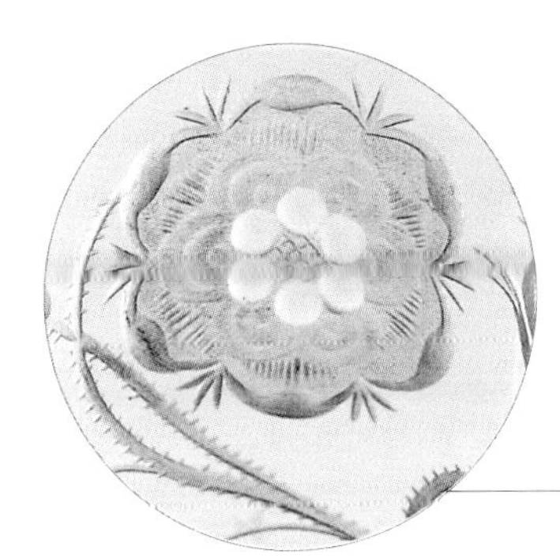

A Jacobite goblet made in 1745 and engraved with a portrait of Prince Charles Edward, a rose, thistles and the Latin phrase "Audentior ibo," *which means "With greater daring shall I go." The glass has long been associated with the Prince and is reputed to have been engraved specially for him to use during a ball held in his honour by the ladies of Edinburgh at Holyrood Palace in 1745. Many later Jacobite glasses were inspired by this form.*

A carriage glass. Used by the passengers travelling inside the coach, these glasses had no foot because there was no place on which to safely lay a glass, such were the state of the roads. Instead, they could be slipped into a small hole at the side of the seat or upturned and set on the floor when they were empty. Poorer passengers sitting on the outside of the coach had to wait for a stop before they could enjoy a drink, and then they, too, would be given a footless glass to empty at speed and return, upturned, to the innkeeper's tray.

This was also the century when industrial innovation began to change the glass industry. Broad glass, made from a cut and flattened cylinder, gradually replaced crown glass for windows. As glass windows became increasingly commonplace, the treasury looked to profit from the trend, and a tax was levied on windows as well as a seven-shillings-per-hundredweight (35p) tax on the raw materials used for glassmaking. The consequences of these taxes were disastrous for some makers: glass output increased by barely two per cent between 1791 and 1828, despite towns in Scotland doubling in size during these years. Not only were duties high, glass was frequently sold by weight until 1822, which provided further disincentive to purchasers. The high costs inevitably resulted in illegal glass trading, and by the end of the century, illicit glass factories could be found in the back streets of many towns.

By the end of the century, the industry was a well-organised affair split into five main types: crown, bottle, broad, plate and flint (or lead crystal). Specialisms were encouraged by statute to protect the various skills. Thus, crystal makers were not permitted to make window glass, and bottle makers were not allowed to make phials holding less than five fluid ounces. The thickness of glass sheets was also determined by law.

From its rather ramshackle beginnings, the glass business expanded and diversified throughout the century. The rapid rise in the importance of glassmaking is amply illustrated by the exports from Glasgow. From having a single bottle works at the beginning of the 18th century, the glass industry there grew at a phenomenal rate. By 1791, when exports were recorded by weight, half a million pounds of common glass, 800,000 pounds of bottles and 31,000 pounds of table glass were exported from the Clyde. Not all of it, of course, was made in the city. Leith too showed an equally dramatic rise in the export of glass to all corners of the globe. As the British Empire grew, so did exports of Scottish glass.

Engraving showing a typical early 19th century glass furnace. It probably measured about six metres across and accommodated nine pots.

Adapted from Pantologia, A new (cabinet) cyclopædia, *1813*

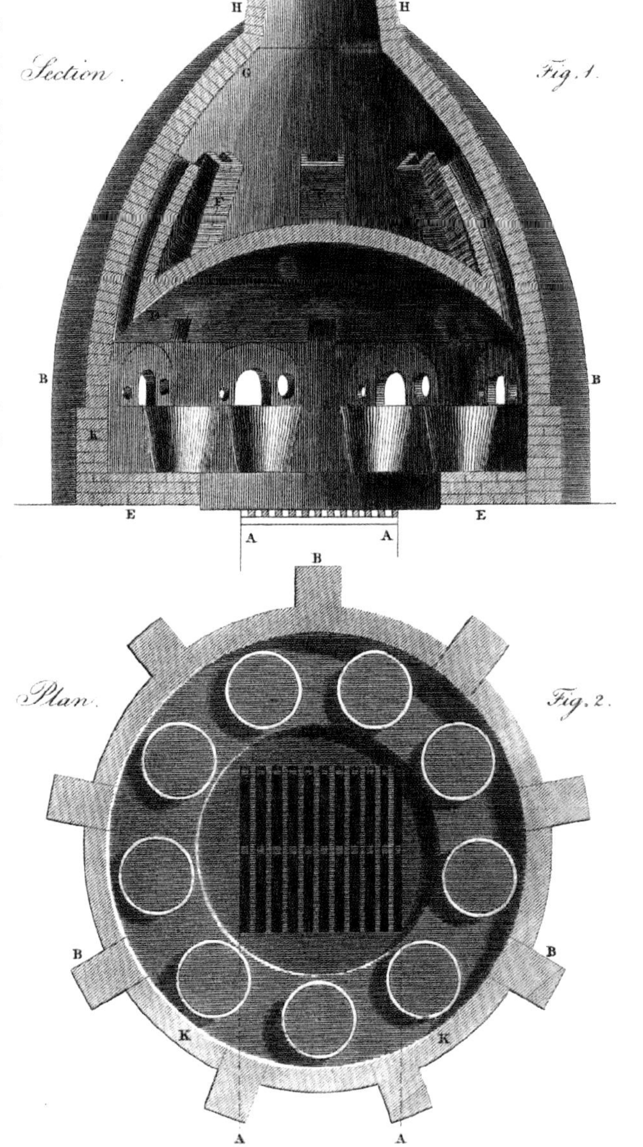

Chapter 3

The 19th Century

The 19th century in Scotland was marked by sharp contrasts. An age of unprecedented industrial advance, it was also the century of Queen Victoria, Sir Walter Scott and an increasingly romantic view of the Highlands. Edinburgh's New Town was complete, and many other Scottish towns had emulated the capital's grand housing plans. But at the same time as the wealthy industrialists lived in splendour, the country was also home to some of the worst slums in Europe. Industrial power may have provided jobs for thousands in Scottish cities, but it did little to improve the living conditions of many of these workers.

The glass industry benefited from both industrial advances and a growing market. Glass objects were no longer bought only by the wealthy, though there remained a market for high-value wares. Innovations in glassmaking introduced increasing mechanisation, so that, by the end of the century, glass had become a mass market product afforded by the many, not the few.

At the beginning of the century, there were thriving and large-scale glassmaking factories in Edinburgh and Glasgow. The Verreville works in Glasgow, having suffered some economic uncertainty, was taken over in 1806 by John Geddes, a former employee of the Edinburgh and Leith Glass Company. He bought it from Mr Dixon, the owner of the Dumbarton Glass Company, who, in an extraordinary business deal had bought the Verreville works and immediately sold it on to Geddes. In an effort to make the company more profitable, and so as not to antagonise Dixon, Geddes stopped making window glass and bottles at the factory and concentrated instead on glasswares.

Trained in glass in Edinburgh by his brother Archibald, the manager of the Leith works, Geddes had also learned as much as he could about chemistry and physics, and employed this knowledge in making glass. He was a true innovator. The first manufacturer in Glasgow to specialise in fine flint table glass, he was also responsible for the introduction of steam power to grind and engrave his glass. The glass he produced was for the top end of the market and included beautifully cut chandeliers and candlesticks, just like those produced by the Ranken family in Leith. Geddes was so successful that he built a mansion in what is now Stobcross Street in Glasgow.

Verreville looked to Irish glass for inspiration, with the result that its wares are often mistaken for Irish work. Derivative it may have been, but Geddes' glass was an immediate success, and he was quick to take advantage of the market by enlarging his product range. A Verreville price list from 1811, which advises that all coloured glass costs two pence (less than 1p) extra per pound weight, lists 25 kinds of drinking glass, 11 kinds of ink pot, 10 different decanters and a whole range of curiosities from nipple covers to lamps, and bird boxes to thermometer tubes.

Geddes also introduced a school to train the glassmakers at his factory. He even trained men to work in other factories, including the one at Alloa, which another family member managed. Verreville was a thriving concern, and its glass cone was a Glasgow landmark until the 1920s, when the works was demolished to make way for a shipping line's engineering works.

The Geddes family also had other interests in Glasgow. John's brother William was a bottle maker at the St Rollox works in Tennant Street in Glasgow. This works was run by the Geddes family until after 1859, by which time it was entitled a flint glass manufacturer, although it continued to make bottles.

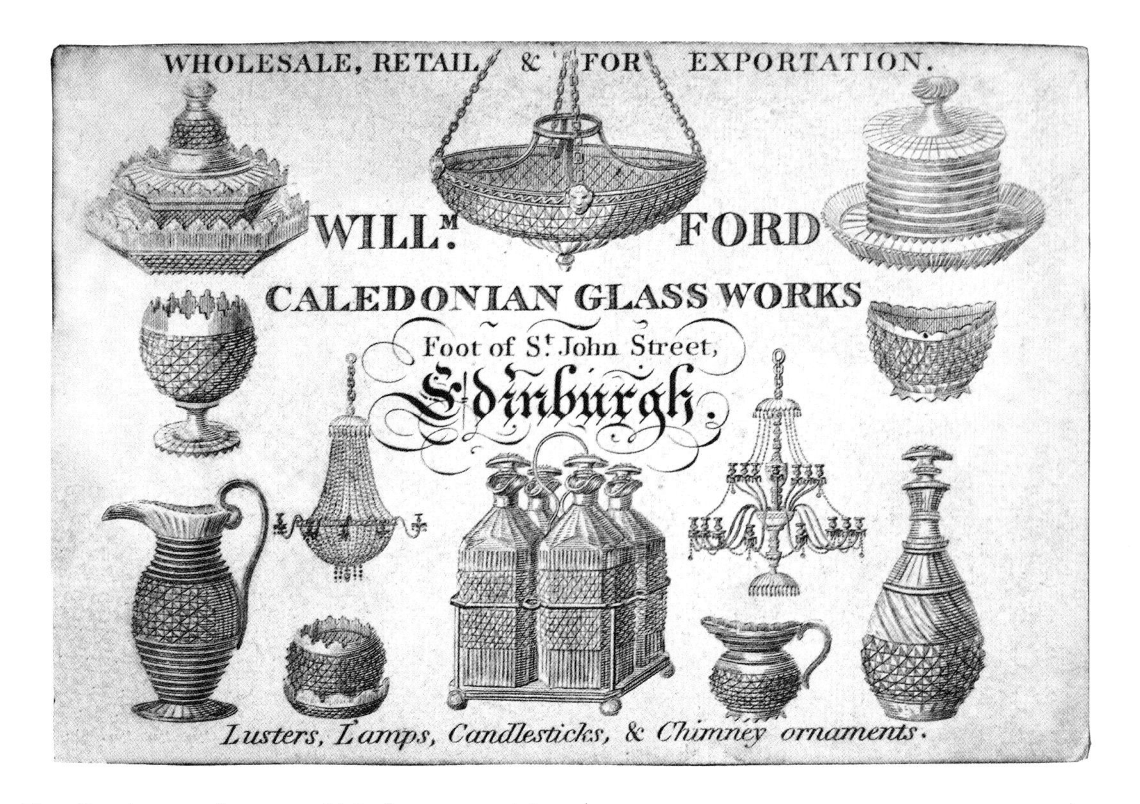

A Caledonian Glassworks advert from 1815.

Copyright © City of Edinburgh Museums and Galleries

The Dumbarton factory, which first opened in 1777 to make bottles, had quickly moved from bottle making into the area of crown glass, and by the beginning of the 19th century was making this to the exclusion of everything else. Under the management of the Dixon family, the factory was the largest of its type in the whole of Britain, and by 1800 it was producing more that 90 per cent of Scotland's crown glass. At the time, it must have been inconceivable to think that the factory would ever fail. However, following the sale of the works to an ironmaster, James Christie, business began to diminish and the factory closed in 1850.

The emergence of Verreville on the west coast appears to have given the Ranken family in Edinburgh little competition. By 1807, John Ranken was making flint glass at the family business in Leith Walk, though it continued to specialise in lustres, girandoles, candlesticks and lamps. The family was still making these items well into the middle of the century, but by that time had moved to Picardy Place, which adjoins Leith Walk. Here, in 1855, Francis Ranken was proudly advertising his "lustres, lamps, girandoles, candlesticks, plain and cut glass in great variety," and even offering lamps on loan for evening parties. The idea of lending glass was certainly a popular one in 19th century Edinburgh. Not everyone could afford expensive lighting like Ranken's, and several local firms offered lamps for hire.

The Leith glassmakers remained a close-knit community at the start of the 19th century. The glassworkers tended to live close to the factory, and other people working in the glass trade lived nearby, so that within a small area one finds mention in the records of stained glass painters, watch glass makers and glass grinders all living in close proximity. The Geddes and Gavine families, managers of the glassworks and the bottle works respectively, dominated this little world well into the century.

In the City of Edinburgh, however, it was not until the opening of the Caledonian Glass Company in 1809 that a glass industry apart from the occasional glass cutter was established. William Ford established the company near the bottom of the Royal Mile. In 1815, the business moved to a former iron foundry in nearby Canongate. Ford died in 1819, and his nephew John Ford leased the factory with some partners. In 1835, John Ford took sole ownership of the business, which he renamed the Holyrood Flint Glass Works. Holyrood glass became such a success that John Ford had to build a larger factory in 1835. The business continued to flourish until 1904, when the family closed it.

John Ford was an inventive glassmaker. He introduced new ranges of glass and exported them all over the world. His diaries and notebooks are filled with jottings about various experiments to produce different colours and types of glass, and it is clear that he was completely absorbed by the technicalities of glassmaking. Some of these experiments bore fruit, and his factory started to make some coloured glass from the 1830s. Between the 1850s and 1880s, it even produced a small range of unusual wares imitating stone, which are frequently confused with French and German glass.

The factory also made a popular range of glass containing cameo inserts. This technique had been developed in England in the 1820s but it was not until the 1880s that the Holyrood factory realised the potential of these objects. The cameo was made of clay set into a mould and partially fired. It was then encased in a tube or blob of glass, ready to be added to a piece of glassware. The cameos were inserted into a wide range of objects, from vases to goblets and commemorative pieces.

In 1855, John Ford was appointed Glassmaker to Her Majesty Queen Victoria, and his works were renamed the Royal Holyrood Glassworks. Victoria obviously liked the glass produced in Edinburgh: she frequently ordered glasses engraved with a view of Balmoral Castle, which she gave as presents.

When John Ford died in 1859, the firm continued to flourish under the management of his sons William and John Humphrey. In 1839, William Ford's daughter had married William Ranken, and John Ford and Company took over the Ranken business in Leith shortly afterwards, although the Rankens retained other premises in Picardy Place and continued to train men in the art of cutting glass. In 1877, William Ford's son-in-law, William Ranken, joined the Ford business, which was so large it now employed about 200 people in the factory.

A wine glass engraved 10 August 1835 to celebrate opening of the new Holyrood Flint Glass Works.

Reputed to be John Ford's apprentice piece, this early 19th century dish has been fashionably cut in the style of Irish glass.

Courtesy Ford Ranken Collection

The Rankens' reputation for fine cut glass continued in Picardy Place and one of their apprentices, Francis R. Sim, was so successful that he had his own chandelier business in Edinburgh's prestigious Princes Street by the mid 19th century. The cut crystal made by the Ford company remained equally desirable and its manufacture continued under William's successor, his son William Ford Ranken. The company kept its close links with the royal family, and in 1898 was honoured with a Royal Warrant and renamed the Royal Holyrood Flint Glassworks. Although the business finally closed in 1904 owing to the unexpected death of the last Ranken, shops that the Ford Rankens had established in the 19th century in London and Edinburgh continued to sell glass well into the 20th century.

If the Ford Ranken dynasty was an important one in Scottish glassmaking, William Bailey was just as influential, founding a bottle business that was to become one of the largest in the country. He began his career as one of John Ford's partners in the Caledonian Glass Company in 1819. Five years later, he set up a bottle works on a site in Portobello, a seaside resort a few miles to the east of the capital. The road where his works and home were located is now called Baileyfield Road in his honour. Bailey had previously been a glassmaker in Newcastle upon Tyne but it was William Ford who assisted him to set up his venture. Although he initially made both vessels and bottles, Bailey concentrated exclusively on bottle making after 1848. Before his death in 1859, he was an influential figure in Portobello and became provost of the town.

When Bailey died in 1859, his managing partner, Richard Cooper, took over the business and renamed it Bailey and Cooper. He then employed his brother-in-law Thomas Wood, a glassmaker from Staffordshire, who remained in partnership with him until 1866. Their bottle business was a great success, and when their partnership was dissolved, Wood retained the existing bottle works, built a new factory at the Baileyfield site and brought a branch

Left: A large "lithyalin" glass vase from the Ford factory and made between 1850 and 1880. This type of coloured glass was designed to imitate semi-precious stones such as agate, and was the pinnacle of Victorian High Fashion.

Second from left to right: A set of "hyalith" glass vases set made in the Ford factory between 1850 and 1880. This dark glass was sold under the name Jasper Ware.

of the nearby railway line right into the works. Like Cooper, he specialised in bottle making, and his factory eventually became the largest bottle works in the country. Wood travelled to Germany and Sweden to learn the latest manufacturing techniques and imported some labour from these foreign factories. He was a true Victorian innovator and introduced water gas to fire his new type of tank furnaces. The factory eventually produced more than eight million bottles a year and employed almost 300 workers.

Not to be outdone, the Cooper family made equally astonishing progress. In 1895, under the management of Thomas Cooper, the company modernised its bottle-making processes, imported German workers and increased its output to six million bottles a year. The Baileyfield site in Portobello continued to be a major supplier of glass bottles until 1968. Bottles made there have been unearthed in excavations all over the world.

Leith's oldest surviving glass factory, the Edinburgh and Leith Glass Company, gradually diversified from making bottles, and by the early 19th century was making a great variety of glasswares. Many of its glasses were cut and engraved and of high quality. Scottish glass frequently looked to the Continent for inspiration, even in the 19th century. Pattern books from the company dating to around 1811 show, amongst other objects, römers with square feet that were based on German glasses. These were high-quality items selling for two shillings and two pence (11p) each. The same books show glasses with threaded bases and some with strawberry prunts – both designs influenced by Continental work. They also took ideas from nearer to home, and made champagne flutes, water jugs and trifle, sugar and water bowls in styles so similar to those of Irish glass that it is easy to mix the two. The situation is further confused by the fact that many glass cutters came to Scotland from Ireland, especially after the famines of the 1840s. The company was still making glass from its new factory in Salamander Street, Leith, at the beginning of the 1870s, although on a much reduced scale and producing only bottles.

This epergne was made at the Holyrood Works to celebrate Queen Victoria's accession to the throne in 1837. It took more than two years to complete, and remains a masterpiece of the glass cutter's art at one metre tall.

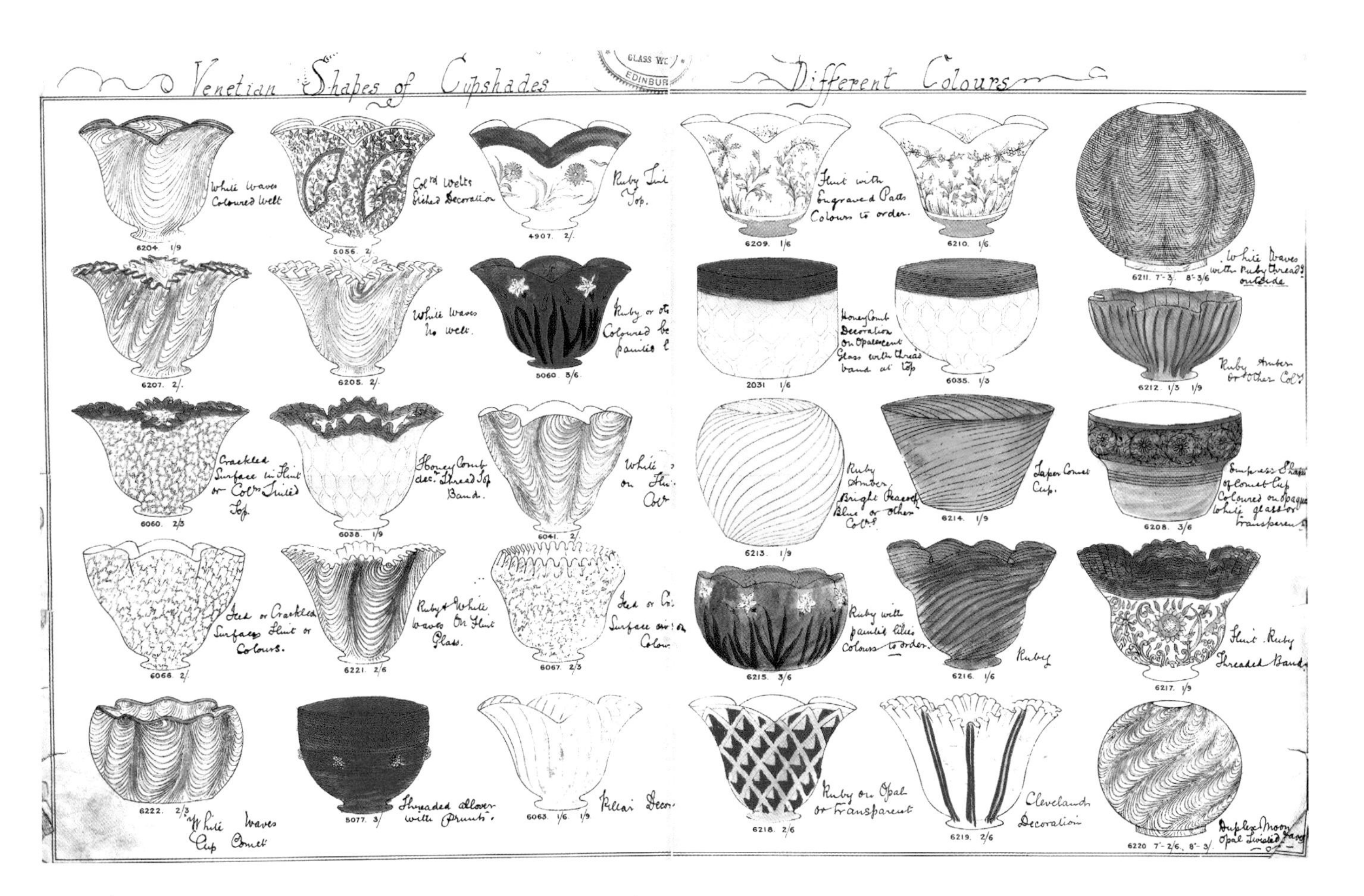

A Holyrood Glassworks design sheet for Venetian bowls. As the century progressed, the company was constantly looking for new designs that reflected the prevailing fashion. Glass in the Venetian style was particularly popular towards the end of the century.

Produced by the Ford factory in the 1880s, this perfume bottle is decorated with a cameo of George Heriot, a 17th century Scottish goldsmith and founder of one of the country's oldest schools, George Heriot's School in Edinburgh.

Courtesy Ford Ranken Collection

A goblet engraved with a view of Balmoral Castle. The Ford company produced these for Queen Victoria to give as presents.

Courtesy Ford Ranken Collection

Around 1850, two more glassmakers also set up a flint glass business in Leith. Opened by John Thomas from London and Leith man Donald Fraser, the business was of sufficient size that by 1851 it employed almost 40 men. Situated on Leith Walk, it was part of what was by now a thriving industry on the east coast. Along with Ford and Ranken, glass was also being manufactured by Frances Sim and James Wood in Edinburgh; in Leith, Thomas and Fraser, and the Edinburgh and Leith Glass Company were flourishing.

Thomas died in 1859, and shortly afterwards the company was taken over and renamed the Edinburgh and Leith Flint Glass Company. It produced an enormous range of glassware, and in 1865 it was sold to the firm of Jenkinson, which moved it to larger premises at Norton Park in Edinburgh in 1876. In the 20th century, this company became Edinburgh Crystal, and its story is told in the next chapter.

Part of the royal wedding service made in 1893 at the Ford factory as the City of Edinburgh's gift to the Duke and Duchess of York, later King George V and Queen Mary. It comprised 256 pieces, which were engraved by Alexander Millar, son of the famous Bohemian glass engraver Joseph Henry Beutlich Millar. Some examples, of which these are a few, were retained by the company.

The importance of Norton Park as a centre of glassmaking was cemented with the arrival of Joseph Henry Beutlich Millar, a Bohemian who emigrated to Scotland around 1859 and set up a workshop as a glass engraver in Norton Place. Many Bohemians left their native countries in the 1850s following political unrest. They made their way across Europe and some of them finally settled in Edinburgh. The Bohemians were skilled craftsmen. Some worked in wood and made furniture, toys and even musical instruments. Others had trained in the Bohemian glass factories, which were renowned for their fine engraving. Millar was one of the best.

Noted for his fine engravings of classical and sporting scenes, he exhibited a three-foot-tall vase engraved with the Battle of Inkerman at the International Exhibition of London in 1862. This magnificent work was purchased by the Duke of Cambridge for 160 guineas (£168). Millar's workshop was a large one and employed almost 40 people. Some were fellow Bohemians who lived close to the workshop, including his son Alexander. But Millar also recruited men from Edinburgh and trained them in the art of engraving. He engraved glass for the Holyrood glassworks but also supplied engraved glass for John Millar and Company. (Grandly titling himself "Potter to Her Majesty," John Millar sold glass and china from a shop in the centre of the city. A Royal Warrant holder, his shop catered for the wealthiest of Edinburgh's citizens.) Millar died in 1879 and his workshop finally closed in 1886. His talented son, Alexander, died of consumption in 1901, aged only 41.

Another talented Bohemian engraver who worked in Scotland at the same time as Millar was Emanuel Lerche, who, having initially worked in Edinburgh, moved to Glasgow in 1873, where he engraved glass for Bailey's works in Alloa until the late 19th century. His fellow countryman H. Keller also worked in Glasgow and produced some of John Baird and Company's finest engraved glass, the quality of which is the equal of Millar's.

But the best engravers of the period were not all Bohemian. John Smith, a Scot, worked beside the Holyrood factory in the 1850s before moving to the Norton Park area in nearby Bangor Road, where he excelled at engraving heraldry on table glass. He

A bottle chip-engraved with the words Janet Stevenson, Grumble Street, Leith 1847. Such bottles were made in huge numbers in the 19th century and it is impossible to know whether this one was made in Leith, Portobello or Alloa, as all the bottle works produced similar wares.

Copyright © City of Edinburgh Museums and Galleries

A moulded bottle bearing the name J&W Petrie, Bathgate. Although it is not known if this was made in Portobello, it is the kind of bottle Cooper and Wood excelled at producing.

Courtesy Bennie Museum, Bathgate

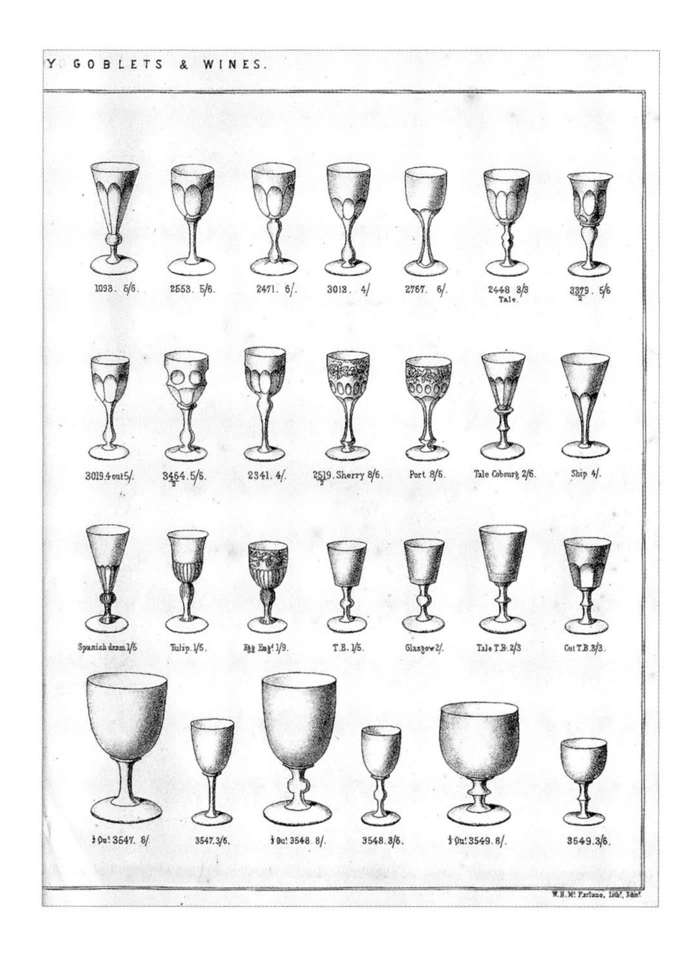

A sample page from an Edinburgh and Leith price list 1868.

gradually expanded his workshop until he employed up to 30 men, all glass cutters, who produced a range of lighting. It was work of the highest order destined for the luxury end of the market. It is indicative of the wealth of Scotland in the later 19th century that so many cutters and engravers found a ready market for their glass.

The factory in Alloa concentrated on bottle making at the beginning of the 19th century. One of its main shareholders at this time was William Geddes, a scion of the Edinburgh glassmaking family. On his death in 1812, his son, William junior, managed the works at Alloa. In 1825, the Geddes family sold its shares in Alloa, though William junior remained as manager until 1850.

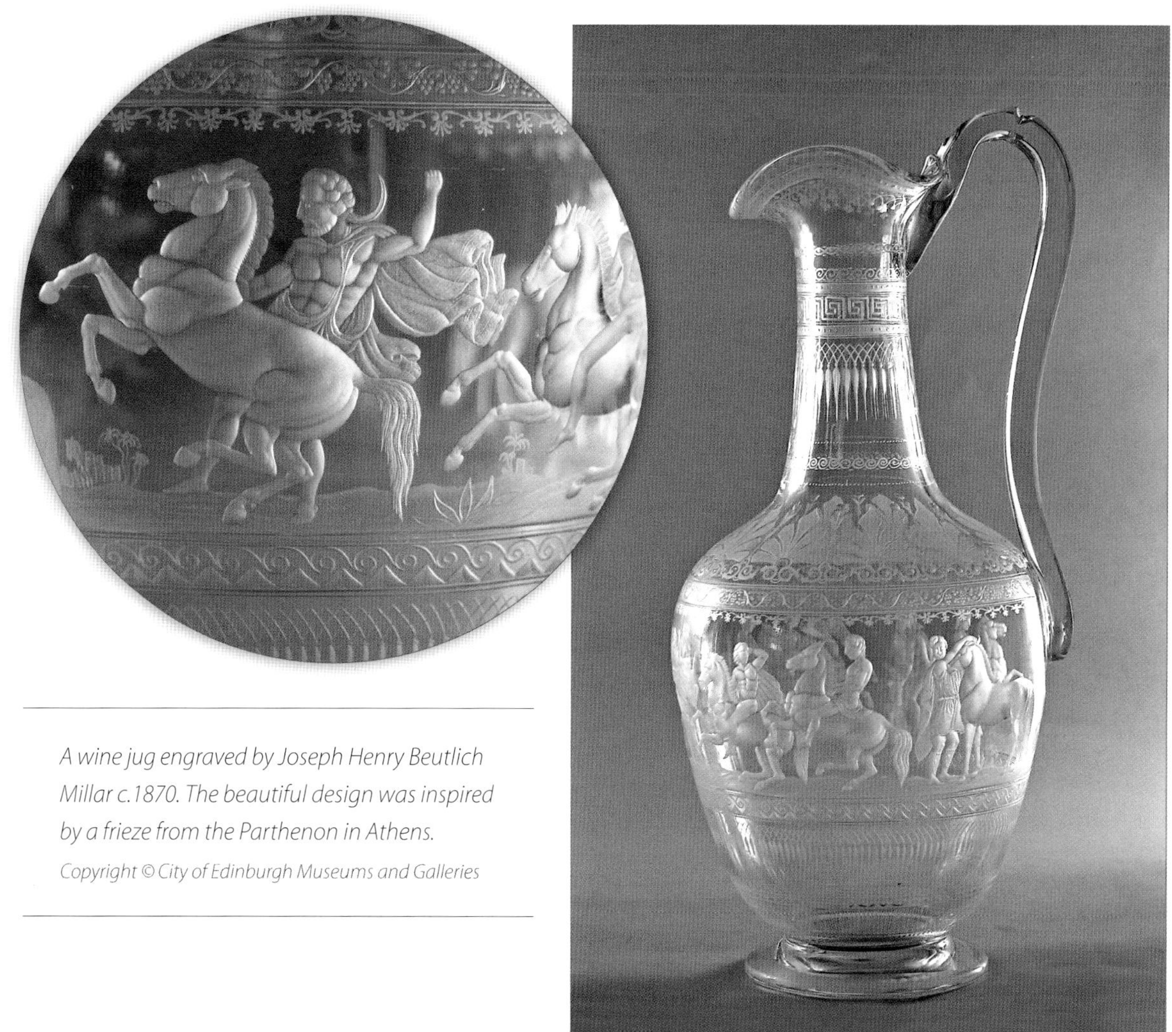

A wine jug engraved by Joseph Henry Beutlich Millar c.1870. The beautiful design was inspired by a frieze from the Parthenon in Athens.

The new owners decided to expand the factory and build additional cones. They also brought in Timothy Warren, a Newcastle-upon-Tyne maker who had trained at the Nailsea factory in Bristol. Warren's expertise enabled the factory to produce table and window glass as well as bottles. This was the time that Alloa glass become famous for its flasks decorated with strips of glass resembling quills. Warren's influence was strong, to the extent that some Alloa and Nailsea glasswares are frequently mistaken for one another.

Around 1832, the business was sold to businessmen from Lanarkshire. They encouraged the making of crown glass, and this quickly became a large part of the business and employed several hundred people. However, having been found guilty of excise evasion in 1839, the company ceased making crown glass and concentrated on bottles instead. Bottle glass was hard, and the Alloa glassmakers were well known for decorating plain bottles by chipping the surface with a sharp hammer. Bottles remained the mainstay of Alloa's output for the rest of the century, and at the beginning of the 20th century it was the first factory in Britain to introduce a mechanised process. As a result of this new technology, Alloa was producing eight million bottles a year by 1914. It became part of United Glass in 1955.

Perth developed a glass industry far later than other Scottish cities: its first glass factory being established before the 1850s. A small-scale affair that used crucibles to melt the glass, it made mainly bottles and later gauge glasses. What was to become a far more important contributor to the glass industry was the Perth enterprise set up in 1865 by John Moncrieff. An ink maker by trade, he built the North British Glassworks initially to make gauge glasses, target balls and ink bottles. Around 1880, he introduced tank furnaces and eventually developed the use of borax in glass to strengthen the gauge glasses. By the beginning of the next century, the company's borosilicate gauge glasses were known around the world, and Moncrieff was to be an important name in the 20th century.

The West Lothian Glass Works was established in the town of Bathgate in 1866. Its founder, Donald Fraser, had been in partnership with John Thomas in Edinburgh. Following Thomas's death and the sale of their works in Leith, Fraser appears to have become a glass merchant in Edinburgh. However, the lure of the furnace was too strong and he resolved to start a new glassmaking business. Set on the site of an old brewery, covering more than an acre and employing 50 workers, this was an ambitious concern from the start. Fraser was determined to produce a wide range of glasswares for the domestic market: everything from gas globes to decanters. His cut and engraved decanters and glasses were particularly popular, and before long Fraser was exporting his glass to the Continent.

An Alloa glass bottle chip-engraved M. Bruce 1851 and decorated with birds, hearts and the Glasgow coat of arms.

Copyright © Culture & Sport Glasgow (Museums)

Mould-blown target balls by Moncrieff. Embossed N. B. [North British] *Glassworks, Perth.*

Copyright © Glass Study Association, France

A white and clear glass flask of the type produced in Alloa.

Courtesy Bennie Museum, Bathgate

When Fraser died in 1869, the Bathgate works was taken over by the Glasgow firm of James Wilson and Sons, who continued Fraser's range, including the popular engraved fern pattern that became the signature design of the factory. Although he still called his factory the West Lothian Flint Glass Works, Wilson diversified into other areas, making glass for use in the chemical industry and introducing the technique of pressing glass. Pressed glass had been invented much earlier in the century, but it was not made in any quantity in Britain until the 1850s. Pressing was to revolutionise the industry, though not without being fiercely opposed by traditional glassmakers, who saw its introduction as a real threat to their skills. Pressing glass required no great skill. A worker simply took a gather of molten glass, pushed it into a mould and applied pressure. It was a quick and cheap way of making identical pieces, and made glassware affordable to even the humblest of households.

In about 1884, the works was taken over by James Couper and Sons of Glasgow, who changed the name to the Bathgate Glass Company. It was now a very large business employing more than 150 workers, but Couper's ownership was to be short-lived. A serious economic depression hit the area in 1887, and the glassworks closed forever.

Pressed glass was not the only invention to revolutionise the glass industry. It was discovered that hydrofluoric acid could be used to etch glass. This is the only acid that eats into glass, and it was soon being used on an industrial scale as a cheaper alternative to engraving. The 19th century is also when plate and, later, sheet glass were developed. In just a few years, the new technology of flat-glass production completely supplanted crown and broad glass for windows. All these developments, along with mechanisation, brought the price of glass down, and by the end of the century, every home owned glass, whether it was a humble bottle or a glass window.

The traditional glassmakers were dismayed by many of these developments, but were powerless to stop them. Their trade society, the Flint Glassmakers' Friendly Society, continued to uphold their traditions, including holding an annual trade parade in towns with a glass industry of any size. One held on 29 July 1831 in Edinburgh was reported in the local press, and was a magnificent affair. The glassmakers from Bailey's and Ford's works paraded evidence of their skills: heralds wore helmets bearing plumes of spun glass, while two enormous crowns, one set with glass jewels, the other bearing the king's cipher, were carried through the streets of the town on spiral staffs of clear crystal. Other makers carried a Scottish thistle surrounded by bluebells, all made from glass; a Chinese pagoda with three tiers of bells; a huge triumphal arch; and eight glass cannons. The grand procession ended at Bailey's showrooms in Greenside Place, where a salvo was fired from the cannons.

Left: A bell-shaped watch stand made in Bathgate and typical of its engraved wares.

Centre: A tumbler decorated with Bathgate's famous fern design (with detail, right).

Right: A pressed-glass jug made at Bathgate.

All photos courtesy Bennie Museum, Bathgate

Just as glassmaking was dominated by a few families in the Edinburgh area, Glasgow also had a close-knit glass community. Several factories produced glass for the chemical industry and other specialist outlets but are beyond the remit of this book. Too many others have faded into obscurity, the glass they produced now unknown. Some from Glasgow are remembered though, like Isaac Rigg and Son who made lustres and chandeliers, which they sold from their shop in Buchanan Street in the middle of the century. Winchester and MacGibbon, who sold wares from nearby Argyle Street during the same period, boasted a far broader range of not only cut and ornamental glass but also "glass vials of all sizes, wine and porter bottles, carboys and chemical utensils." However, two companies dominated the domestic glass market: John Baird and James Couper.

James Couper set up the City Flint Glassworks in Kyle Street, Glasgow, with two of his sons in 1850. The three-acre site housed a showroom as well as the factory. Couper was a retailer, and this training made him determined from the start that the factory should produce a range of table glass, not only for homes but also for hotels and ships. His modern, well-equipped factory made use of all the latest technology. Couper's glass was etched using a sand-blasting technique, and he also introduced machine etching using a pantograph, thus effectively mass producing decorated glass, although he also had ranges that were engraved by traditional methods using a grinding wheel. By the 1860s, Couper's output of sherry, wine and port glasses had been supplemented with a range that included chandeliers. The company also advertised a range of "coloured enamelled and gilded glass of every description." Before long, Couper had diversified into producing lighting of all types, and he made a coloured-glass electric light fitting for the Queen's residence at Sandringham in Norfolk, as well as those in Glasgow's City Chambers.

Couper positively embraced new technology. His retail instincts urged him to develop an increasingly wider range of products, and, by the time of his death in 1884, the company was making an enormous number of specialised glasses for the chemical industry, toughened glass for steam gauges and even lenses for lighthouses. He died the year his company took over the glassworks in Bathgate and it fell to his grandson, aged only 19, to continue the family business.

A pressed-glass plate made for the 1888 Glasgow Exhibition. Thousands of commemorative plates were made in the Victorian era using the pressed-glass process. Although most were produced in England, Scots seem to have taken a particular liking to them. This design is still a treasured possession in many Scottish households and often makes an appearance at Hogmanay laden with shortbread or black bun.

Haden Richardson Couper was named after William Haden Richardson, the Stourbridge glassmaker appointed works manager at the City Flint Glassworks in 1858. Haden Couper's main interest was in producing coloured and textured glass. There was a growing market for stained glass, and James Couper and Sons had introduced the St Mungo range in about 1855 to meet this demand. With its wide variety of rich colours, which later included various textures, the range became a prominent feature in many churches nationwide. It also appeared in the villas of the merchants and businessmen who were, in the latter part of the century, building houses away from Glasgow's grimy industrial centre in the cleaner suburbs to the south, west and north.

Almost certainly, it was Haden who introduced the use of coloured glass for tablewares at the company. His sample collection in Glasgow Museums and Art Galleries includes chemicals probably used in colour experiments, samples of gathers and whole or part crown-glass discs. There are also examples of miniature vases and other glass ornaments.

It is not known for certain how Christopher Dresser, one of the most famous names in 19th century design and a major influence in the 20th century, and, later, architect and designer George Walton became associated with Couper's. Family tradition has it that Haden's elder brother, James Couper III (sometime known as Tertius) introduced Dresser to the company. But both men were Glaswegians. Both had reacted against the florid mid-Victorian fashions in interior design. Both designed in a wide variety of fields: ceramics, furniture, textiles and glass, for example.

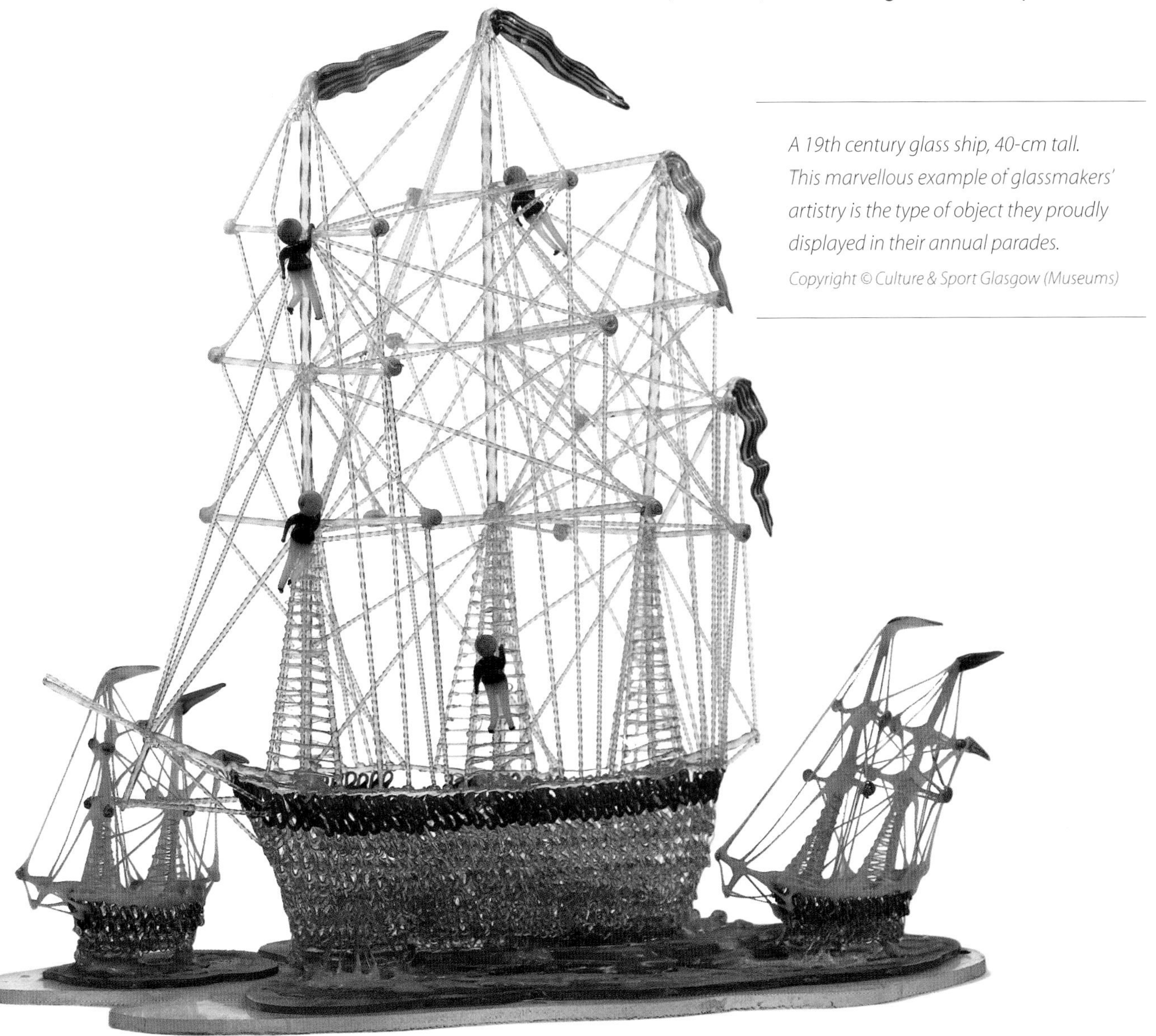

A 19th century glass ship, 40-cm tall. This marvellous example of glassmakers' artistry is the type of object they proudly displayed in their annual parades.

Dresser in his *Principles of Decorative Design* had insisted that glassworkers should, as far as possible, allow the molten glass to shape itself according to "natural laws" after the act of blowing, and that objects should, above all, display "fitness for purpose," i.e., they should work. He considered the then current fashion for deep cutting to be abhorrent, though he did not object to coloured glass and admired the softness and delicacy of Roman and Greek glass. In practice, many of his designs, whether in glass or ceramic, do not conform strictly to his theories, as they often indicate exotic sources such as Central American ceramic shapes. Many items of the Clutha glass range that Couper's produced in the last two decades of the 19th century demonstrate his theories.

In June 1888, Arthur Lazenby Liberty registered the name Clutha in simple sans-serif capitals under the Patents, Designs, and Trade Marks Act, 1883, and the following December, a J. C. & S. monogram within a trilobal shape was registered by James Couper and Sons. These marks appear on a variety of shapes of glass, coloured in various tones of brown and green, often shaded and sometimes with aventurine inclusions.

The association of the Couper's with Liberty & Co., the London department store, is also unexplained, but it is likely that Dresser, who at this time had designed textiles for the retailer, might have recommended the Glasgow firm as a source of interesting glass.

An engraved champagne glass made about 1870 by James Couper and Sons.

Above: Three jars containing chemicals used to colour glass and used by Haden Richardson Couper.

Below: Glass showing Haden Richardson Couper's experiments with coloured glass, probably designed for stained-glass makers.

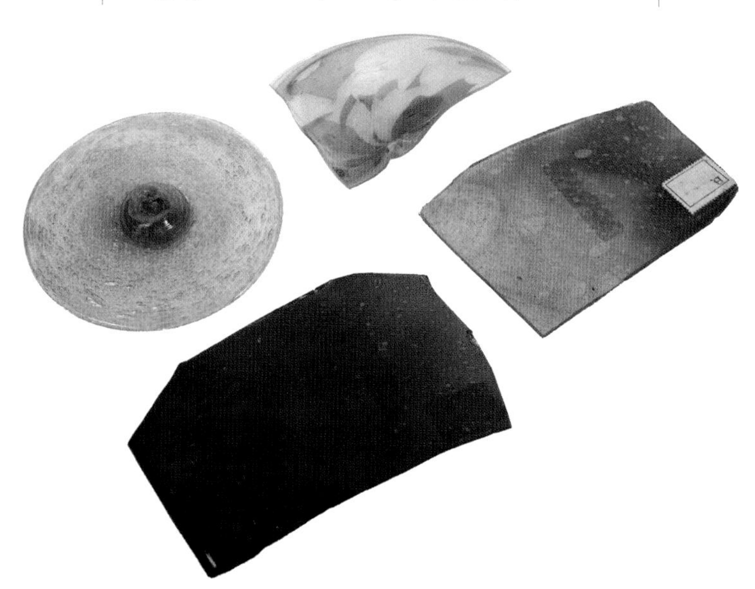

Window probably designed by Haden Richardson Couper for a mansion in Pollokshields.

Courtesy Brian Blench

Walton's work for the firm is subtly different to Dresser's; it is more restrained in form and more geometric yet it retains the feeling of freedom that characterised the work of his predecessor.

Two of Walton's sisters, Helen and Hannah also made a small contribution to Scottish glassware at the time. Helen had trained at the Glasgow School of Art, as it was named by then, and gave classes in drawing and painting in her studio at the family home in Hillhead. She also taught china and glass decoration. Hannah developed a particular facility in this type of work, and the sisters carried out collaborative work for many years, almost certainly using blanks from Couper's and Baird's. This sort of work, along with similar decorative work on glazed but plain ceramics, was a popular pastime for genteel ladies well into the 20th century.

Above: The Clutha trademark.

Courtesy Brian Blench

Below: Some typical glass from the Clutha range, probably designed by Christopher Dresser.

Copyright © Culture & Sport Glasgow (Museums)

One of the most intriguing glass companies to be founded in Glasgow in the later 19th century was John Baird and Company. Baird trained as a glass silverer, or mirror maker, and in 1876 he appears to have set up a works in Port Dundas in Glasgow with the intention of specialising in mirror making. That arm of the business was a success, and he exported mirrors all over the world. Before long, however, he had diversified into making gauge and scientific glass. For a short period, Baird also produced some domestic glass. Quite how he made the leap from mirror and scientific glass is not known, but in the 1880s, his company was producing some of the finest drinking glasses and wine jugs to be found in Glasgow. The quality is the equal to that of the best glass produced in Edinburgh, and Baird was aiming at the upper end of the market when he made it. Some of this glass was engraved by H. Keller, a Bohemian engraver. This beautiful glass was perhaps too expensive to be a successful range, and Baird seems to have made it for only a short time before reverting to more profitable lines, such as adverts on glass, but it marks a high point of glassmaking in the city.

A Baird advertising weight.

Courtesy Broadfield House Glass Museum

A wine jug with matching glasses made by John Baird and Company, and finely engraved by H. Keller in around 1886 with a romantic design of birds and wreaths.

Copyright © Culture & Sport Glasgow (Museums)

A late 19th century print of the cutting and engraving room at Holyrood Flint Glass Works.

If the 19th century began with a flourish of new glass factories, it ended in a turmoil of technological advance. Glassblowers and cutters were still in demand, but faced stiff competition from pressed glass. The skills of the bottle maker were about to be lost forever as machines took their place and produced millions of absolutely perfect, standard bottles. Makers of window glass were also a dying breed, gradually being replaced by techniques that did not require their mastery of the glassblower's art. The glass industry in Scotland was about to change forever.

Jug decorated by the Walton sisters with appropriate watery theme, along with similar glass items.

Commonwealth links

An amusing little anecdote came to light from a glass enthusiast in Canada as this book was going to press.

The decanter shown in the photographs dates from late 19th century and was made by Jenkinson, which became the Edinburgh and Leith Flint Glass Company, and later Edinburgh Crystal. It was made at a time when Jenkinson had brought glassblowers over from Murano to help the company to diversify its product range. However, the experiment in the change of style was eventually discontinued, perhaps because they did not particularly appeal to the company's customers.

The decanter belongs to David Fisher of Surrey, British Columbia, Canada, whose uncle, Robert Jack, gave it to him. Robert worked as a glass cutter for Edinburgh and Leith Flint Glass before emigrating to Canada after World War II in 1948. He was given the piece by his father, who, along with his grandfather, also worked for the company. David's uncle told him that one aunt had had a cupboard full of similar items, including some *reticello* work, but as she did not like it as much as cut crystal, she threw it all out.

David's aunt Ann Jack, one of the sharpest people he knows, was told in the 1930s that the white parts in the decanter came from seagull feathers melted in glass. She was taken in enough to repeat the story to David, whose quick smile forced him to fill her in about "feathering" and glass.

Robert took his cutting wheel to Canada, and, initially repaired crystal for Woodward's, a local chain of department and grocery stores, before he became manager of one of their smaller stores. He also cut anything he could get his hands on. He managed to get hold of blank Thistle whisky glasses from Edinburgh Crystal, and cut David and other nieces and nephews a set, each with an individual pattern. He even collected empty jam jars to work on, and displayed these throughout his basement. He continued cutting glass until he had a stroke in the mid 1990s.

Once a glassworker, always a glassworker.

Feathered effect

The feathered effect is called *vetro fenicio* in Murano. It is achieved by running a metal comb (a *maneretto*) over applied lines of glass (canes) and then rolling the gather on the marver to flatten them. The word *fenicio* comes from Phoenician, as the effect was developed in that ancient civilization.

With thanks to David Fisher

A decanter, with a fenicio, *or feathered, effect and a cut crystal claret jug, both Jenkinson late 19th century. The neck of the decanter was repaired many years ago, as was common with prized possessions.*

Chapter 4

The 20th Century and Beyond

One of the world's best-known names in 20th century Scottish glass is that of Edinburgh Crystal. The company was for many decades an epitome of quality and a stalwart of many wedding gift lists, but it had passed its peak of innovation by the mid 20th century.

When Alexander Jenkinson took over the Leith Walk glassworks of the Edinburgh and Leith Flint Glass Company in 1865 he already had wide knowledge of the china and glass trade from the retail side. The works had a reputation for producing high-quality wares, and had exhibited ornamental glass at the London International Exhibition of 1862 and the 1867 Exposition Universelle in Paris, France, where the jury praised both the quality of the engraving and the clarity of the glass. However, the premises were cramped, so a new works with 12 pot furnaces opened in 1876 in Norton Park adjacent to the Edinburgh, Leith and Granton branch of the North British Railway.

Jenkinson introduced new ranges: notably Venetian-style tablewares often with coloured glass additions or inclusions, and crystal with cut or engraved decoration. Within two years, the company again exhibited at the Exposition Universelle to high praise from the jury.

In the later decades of the 19th century, the company developed a range of lighting wares to meet the expanding demand for both gas and electric light shades – just as Couper had done so successfully in Glasgow. In the 20th century, however, it was with the development of high-quality crystal decorated with deep and intricate cut patterns that it became most associated.

A Jenkinson cocktail glass and a finger bowl in the Italian style with applied thistles – a combination of the old and the new. These show the contrast between the traditional Venetian-style wares and one of the newer shapes. This may be one of the earliest cocktail glasses made in Scotland.

In 1909, Stanley Noel Jenkinson, Alexander's grandson and the last of the family connected with the firm, took over. He was a founder member of the Society of Glass Technology and became its president in 1919. He had particular interests in research into refractories and in technical glass. These interests proved invaluable during World War I when the factory had to produce materials for the war effort: tubing, laboratory glass, light bulbs and other specialist apparatus. During this period, wages fell and men enrolled in or were conscripted to the armed forces. Consequently, there was a shortage of labour, so Stanley Jenkinson recruited workers from Europe. The most notable of these was Salvador Ysart, who, with his family, would become a major player in the development of the Scottish glass industry for over 50 years from the 1920s onwards.

The company was one of the first glassworks to return to normal production after 1918, but Webb's Crystal Glass Co. Ltd of Stourbridge acquired it soon after in 1921. The production of cut glasswares continued during the 1920s with technical improvements such as the use of acid polishing to restore the brilliance of the glass after cutting. The designs were, however, less innovative, though they did include the famous Thistle service, which remained a mainstay of production for decades. Reproductions of Jacobite glass were also made, and in the 1930s, items of clear glass shading into various colours were developed.

The outbreak of war in 1939, as in 1914, interrupted normal production. This time, the major products for the war effort were components for radar equipment and the glass envelopes for cathode ray tubes. Regular production resumed very quickly in 1945, though a new generation of artisans needed training; much of this effort devolved on the cutting and engraving shop supervisor, Fred Lonie. In 1952, the works produced pressed glassware for the first time.

In 1955, the company was renamed The Edinburgh Crystal Glass Company, but it was becoming clear that a new name was not enough to sustain the business properly. The factory site was unsuitable for further development, so a new site was needed. This became possible when Crown House acquired the company in 1964, and then merged it and Thomas Webb & Sons with Dema Glass, another Crown House subsidiary, two years later.

Left: The Thistle service consisted of a decanter and six glasses. It featured both engraving and cutting, and was first produced in about 1895. It was reintroduced in the 1920s as pattern number H828.

Copyright © City of Edinburgh Museums and Galleries

Below: Edinburgh Crystal's Mirror design range featured mitre-cut panels with polished ovals. The bucket vase is in Golden Amber.

Photography Chael Merika, Washington Chase Collection

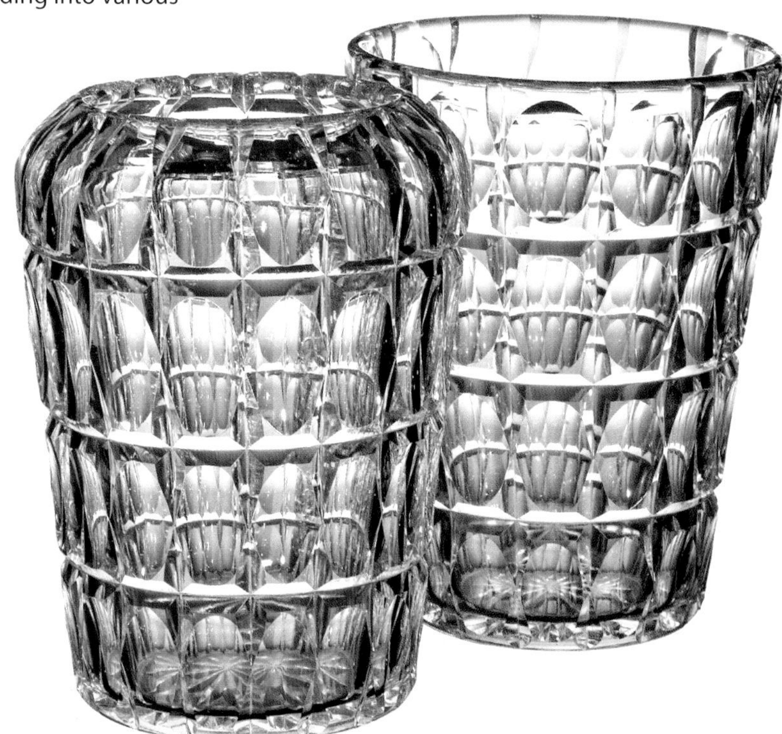

Eventually, the Norton Park works was partially cleared, and new premises with an 11,000-ft^2 cutting shop were established on a seven-and-a-half-acre site at Penicuik, 10 miles to the south of Edinburgh. The cold-end processes of cutting, engraving, polishing, packing and warehousing moved there in 1969, while glassmaking continued at Norton Park. There were trials using butane gas rather than oil for the furnaces before the hot processes too moved to the new factory in 1974. Glassmaking had finally left Edinburgh.

View of the Penicuik works from an advertisement from about 1964.

The company continued production over the next three decades but there was little innovation. Public tastes were changing, and there was increasing competition from abroad and within the UK. Competition was particularly strong from rivals such as Waterford Crystal and Stuart Crystal. Despite the acquisition of Caithness Glass and Selkirk Glass in an attempt to broaden its commercial base, by 2004 losses were running at £1 million a year. The Edinburgh Crystal Glass Company went into liquidation in 2006. Edinburgh Crystal remains solely a brand name.

One family above all dominated the development of art glassmaking in Scotland during the middle decades of the 20th century – the Ysarts. Salvador Ysart, the son of a glassmaker, was born in Barcelona, Spain, in 1878, and he started work in the local glassworks before he was 10. In 1909, he moved to France, attracted by the thriving art glasshouses around Nancy. He worked for various companies, including Schneider Frères et Wolf at Epinay-sur-Seine. This factory closed soon after the outbreak of World War I, but the following year one of Jenkinson's agents for the Leith Flint Glass Company recruited Salvador to help train glassblowers to meet the growing demand for electric light bulbs. So he moved to Edinburgh with his family, which included four sons: Paul, Augustine, Vincent and Antoine.

In 1916, the family relocated to Glasgow, where Salvador worked at the St Rollox works of A. & R. Cochran Ltd for six years until the factory closed down. He then moved to Perth and joined John Moncrieff Ltd to make laboratory wares with Paul as his apprentice.

For centuries, employers have allowed their glassmakers to make friggers – glass objects, usually decorative items such as glass ships and other ornaments, made from the metal remaining in the pot at the end of a shift. Isobel Moncrieff, wife of the owner of the Moncrieff works, noticed one such item, which a local minister had received for a church raffle. This was a vase made with coloured enamels that Salvador had brought from France. Mrs Moncrieff encouraged Salvador to experiment with designs for coloured domestic items. Of artistic bent herself, she also contributed ideas for shapes and colours. By 1924, the company was ready to market Monart Ware, although on a made-to-order basis.

Monart vase in blue and lilac striped bubble glass, shape WC.
Courtesy Glass Study Association, France

Green balluster vase with dark green swirls of green aventurine. shape RA.
Photography Chael Merika, Washington Chase Collection

A sample page from a Monart Ware pattern book. Retailers could select which items they wished to purchase.

Courtesy Glass Study Association, France

MODELS

AA BA CA

DA EA FA

GA HA IA

JA KA LA

MA

JOHN MONCRIEFF LIMITED PERTH SCOTLAND

MONART HAND MADE GLASS

As with Clutha glass some years before, the wide range of objects, including vases, bowls, lampshades, ink bottles, candlesticks, scent bottles, decanters, thimbles and ashtrays with their brilliant colouring and restrained geometric shapes, was an immediate commercial success. By the early 1930s, the range of wares was finalised and the company issued two pattern books from which retailers could select many shapes and sizes.

During this period, all four Ysart sons were their father's apprentices, and they worked as a team, from time to time returning to making laboratory wares as the production needs of the main factory demanded. However, the outbreak of World War II stopped production of all Moncrieff items but those for the war effort.

After the war, during which time Antoine died in a cycling accident, the company was reluctant to restart full production of Monart Ware. In the climate of austerity after the war, the purchase tax on such luxury goods, even if their production were allowed, would have made them very expensive. Production was intermittent and in the family's spare time between 1939 and 1947. However, Paul Ysart did produce a 33-piece set of tableware in mottled pale blue with aventurine inclusions as a gift from the city of Perth for the marriage of Princess Elizabeth to Prince Phillip of Greece and Denmark in 1947.

Paul continued to produce Monart Ware until 1961, the year of Mrs Moncrieff's death. However, he had become more and more interested in making paperweights, so in 1962, he accepted a new challenge as the technical adviser and training officer of the newly established Caithness Glass at Wick.

Left: The Vincent Ysart Vase was made by Vincent Ysart as a gift for his wife, Catherine, in the 1950s. This is the only known example of this type of decoration: yellow and dark grey glass enlivened by multicoloured filigree canes.

Perth & Kinross Council, photograph copyright © Ivo Haanstra

Right: A Paul Ysart paperweight and, in detail, the location of the PY cane.

Copyright © Culture & Sport Glasgow (Museums

In 1946, Salvador, Augustine and Vincent left Moncrieff and established their own factory, Ysart Brothers, at the Shore Works, Perth, where they began the production of Vasart ware. Their production closely resembled Monart Ware, although the colour range was more limited, and softer and more subtle, because of restricted supplies from Eastern Europe, the source of the brightly coloured enamels. The company also obtained contracts to produce decorated advertising glassware from Pirelli Glass of Potters Bar in England. In 1956, George Dunlop of Pirelli Glass joined them, and, together, they set up Vasart Glass Ltd. By this time, they had added traditional paperweights to their range.

Four years later, Stuart Drysdale, a local lawyer, became the manager of the company. Among the company's most attractive wares were small ashtrays and bowls with wavy-edged rims, miniature vases and posy baskets of various sizes.

In 1963, the company received an order from the Prime Minister, Scot and former earl Sir Alec Douglas-Home, for lighting globes for 10 Downing Street. He was trying to encourage industry in his largely rural constituency, Kinross and Perthshire. (Douglas-Home had renounced his peerage in order to enter the Commons, as he felt that it was impractical to serve as Prime Minister from the Lords.) The order was for 20 large globes for the Cabinet Room at 10 Downing Street and 135 of varying sizes for other rooms in 10–12 Downing Street. The smaller globes presented no problem, but the larger globes required 11 men to move them. They had been priced at £150 each but actually cost £400 to produce. Though prestigious, the commission proved a financial disaster. The company was down to a handful of employees, the works was in a dilapidated condition and closure seemed imminent.

Also in 1963, Adam Bergius, then export director of whisky distiller Wm Teacher & Sons Ltd, was in New York where he saw a curiously deformed whisky bottle that an inquisitive potter had placed in his cooling kiln overnight: he had wanted to see what would happen. By the morning, the bottle had collapsed and settled into a shape suitable for nuts or nibbles, or even as an ashtray. Bergius thought it might make a curious and original advertising gimmick.

On his return to the UK, Bergius showed the bottle to several glass manufacturers to see if they could reproduce the experiment in large numbers. No one felt that they could, or would, be able to do it. It was finally shown to the Vasart factory where Vincent, after several attempts during 1963, developed a method and designed a special kiln for the job. The condition of the works meant that only a few, about 120 a week, could be produced. This was not enough in the long term; Teacher's demand had risen to perhaps 60,000 a year. The decision was that Wm Teacher would take over the Vasart firm and build a completely new works.

Vasart bucket vase in Harlequin pattern with orange body.

Photography Chael Merika, Washington Chase Collection

Collapsed Teacher's whisky bottles. The one in the centre is from the first batch produced at the Vasart factory; the two outer ones are probably from the Strathearn factory.

Copyright © Glass-Study Association, France

In April 1964, Wm Teacher & Sons Ltd became the major shareholder in Vasart. By December that year, the new works had been designed and built on the banks of the River Earn on the outskirts of Crieff: the first glassworks in Europe to use propane gas for firing its furnaces. The formal opening of Strathearn Glass Ltd by the Right Honourable Sir Alec Douglas-Home took place in February 1965, though public funds had not been used.

The chief glassmaker at Strathearn was David Moir from Vasart. Vincent Ysart was the first works manager, although he left glassmaking forever later in 1965, and Stuart Drysdale was the general manager. The board of the new company included Angus Sillars who very quickly became managing director.

Though Sillars had no previous experience of the glass industry, he had attended evening classes at Glasgow School of Art, and he proved to be an innovative designer for Strathearn. He learned both the theory and the practice of glassmaking and forming. Untrammelled by tradition, he caused a stir among some of the glassmakers by designing crystal that included crushed quartz or granite, when they had tried so hard to keep the crystal pure.

The Strathearn trademark, a leaping salmon.

Supplies of colour had become easier to obtain, and Sillars modified some of the basic Vasart shapes to produce a strongly coloured range of vases and bowls, and introduced new shapes. Production also included clear glass for engraving, and in 1973, the Strathearn engraving workshop opened under the direction of Alasdair Gordon, a graduate of Edinburgh College of Art (ECA). The studio specialised in commemorative and commissioned pieces, though there was also a standard range of subjects. Gordon emigrated to Australia in 1980, and Sheona Wilson took over the direction of the studio. The manufacture of paperweights, initially very like those produced at Vasart but that gradually evolved into distinct Strathearn styles, was another aspect of the company's operation.

Early Strathearn wares designed by Angus Sillars and exhibited at the first international exhibition of handmade glass (Exposição Vidro Manual), which was held at the National Institute for Industrial Investigation (Instituto Nacional de Investigação Industrial), Lisbon, Portugal, in 1972. The group includes some of the clear glass with inclusions that dismayed the more traditional glassmakers at the factory.

When Wm Teacher became part of Allied Breweries in 1976, the quantity of promotional bottles required was one that Strathearn could not supply. By the early 1980s, demand for highly coloured glass had declined and the works faced closure. Discussions with Stuart & Sons Ltd of Stourbridge followed, and a new company, Stuart Strathearn, was established in 1981. This was to be run by a workers' association, to occupy the premises rent-free and to continue producing glassware and also blanks for cutting in Stourbridge. Two new furnaces were installed at that time, and paperweight production ceased. All production at the works ended in 1991.

World War II had drastic effects on normal glass production for the domestic market, but a college department created, surprisingly, during that period and its graduates were major factors in the regeneration of the glass industry in Scotland in the second half of the 20th century. That department was the Department of Glass Design, under Helen Monro Turner, at ECA.

Annie Helen Nairn Monro was born in December 1901 in Calcutta, India, where her father was working as a newspaper editor. She came to Edinburgh as a child and was educated at George Watson's Ladies College. After taking an arts degree at Edinburgh University she proceeded to ECA, where she specialised in wood engraving, and received her diploma, with commendation, in 1927.

Helen Monro in about 1940 working at her engraving lathe, which came from the Holyrood Glassworks.

Courtesy Brian Blench

While still at the college, Monro visited the Edinburgh and Leith Flint Glass Works and filled a sketchbook with drawings of the workers (1926). By 1929, she was illustrating publicity material for the company. She also submitted designs for glass decoration and objects to the company. Several still survive with comments such as, "This cannot be done. It has never been done before.... This is too new, too unfamiliar. It will not sell." As she wrote later, "it was a frustrating time."

Glass sandblasted and engraved with The Dancers. Inscribed on the base "To D.L.M." Made in Stuttgart in 1938 by Helen Monro.

Courtesy Brian Blench

Advertisement for Edinburgh Crystal by Helen Monro Turner.

Courtesy Denis Hebden

Her frustration no doubt increased in 1930 when the Royal Society of Arts design competition commended one of her designs. In 1935, the Edinburgh and Leith Flint Glass Works even included examples of her work, along with that of three other graduates, the Misses Mungall, Hewatt and Trainer, in the Royal Academy of Arts publication *A Survey of British Industrial Art,* which purported to showcase the best of contemporary design. Perhaps some of her designs were too complicated to be marketable and occasionally too traditional, but then so were the company's products.

The publishing industry, particularly the Edinburgh publisher Thomas Nelson and Sons, appreciated the quality of Monro's engraving and her imaginative use of the medium more. For 40 years from 1933, she illustrated educational and recreational books for children, and produced illustrations and cover designs for other books. The Edinburgh and Leith Flint Glass Works used some of her striking art deco designs for price lists and advertisements but not for its products.

When, in 1938, the ECA elected Monro to an Andrew Grant Travelling Fellowship, her interest in glass had not diminished, so, on the advice of Professor William Turner, head of the Department of Glass Technology at Sheffield University, she decided to study at the Kunstgewerbeschule in Stuttgart, Germany, under Professor Wilhelm von Eiff. There, she studied a wide variety of glass-decorating techniques and engraving of all types.

In her diary, she wrote that on arrival there followed 10 months of "intensive work, learning glass cutting and engraving, and the use of the hand drill on glass.... There were periods of depression when I felt that this task of learning glass techniques personally was too big to have attempted in so little time, though I was sure that it was fundamental for a designer. In the end, I was glad to find that I had made more progress than I had dared to hope for." She was also able to see some of the German countryside, and there were visits to glass factories and studios in Germany and Austria. On 14 August 1939, she decided: "...when term ended at Stuttgart it seemed advisable to be on the other side of the frontier, and I left Stuttgart for Zurich."

Left: A bowl designed by Helen Monro in 1935, made at the Edinburgh and Leith Flint Glassworks, and exhibited at Burlington House, London, home to the Royal Academy.

Courtesy Brian Blench

Windows on the staircase of National Library of Scotland deep sandblasted by Helen Monro Turner assisted by John Lawrie.

Coptright © David P. Encill
Courtesy of National Library of Scotland

Back in Edinburgh, Monro opened a studio at 50 Queen Street, and, with her fellowship renewed, visited glass collections, factories and other places and people of glass interest. This occupied much of 1940: the year the authorities at the college invited her to start a class in glass engraving. On 8 January 1941, she began teaching with four students and two lathes in a basement studio.

For the next 30 years, Monro pursued three careers, as a graphic artist, as a glass engraver and as a teacher. Despite this workload, she made annual visits to Norway between 1947 and 1951 to instruct trainee engravers and so help in the reconstruction of the glass industry there, which had been virtually destroyed during the German occupation.

On 1 July 1943, Monro married Professor Turner and became known as Helen Monro Turner. She had expressed a desire to wear something of glass for her wedding, so she wore a mid-blue, full-length fibreglass dress, with matching handbag, shoes and hat, to the ceremony at St Giles' Cathedral in Edinburgh. Glass Fibres Ltd of Glasgow, a subsidiary of Chance Brothers, which had taken over the Glasgow Plate Glass Company in 1907, made the fabric used. The company was renamed Fibreglass Ltd in 1944 and closed in 1964.

In 1947, Monro Turner became a full-time instructor in the college, and the department slowly expanded. John Lawrie, a former student, assisted her in much of this development.

Monro Turner's reputation as a glass engraver spread rapidly, and she received constant requests for items for presentations and anniversaries, which left little time for speculative work or exhibitions. Consequently, most of her output remains in private hands and there are few items in public collections. The scale of her work ranged from a single glass or a tiny engraved crystal box to huge architectural commissions such as the windows on the staircase of the National Library of Scotland. For every one, there was a period of research before she produced precise design drawings, each consummate works of art.

As a teacher, her declared aim was "to communicate enthusiasm...(for) the best work is done *con amore*... the final principle into which all other rules resolve themselves is quite literally love of the work, an act of devotion, a practice of the art of giving, which is indeed the first principle of the art of living."

The name Department of Glass Design was a considered choice, as it was Monro Turner's ambition that it should not concentrate solely on glass engraving but should eventually cover all aspects of glassmaking and decoration.

By 1953, the department had more space, five lathes, two cutting lathes and sandblasting equipment. In the early years, students travelled to Stourbridge for instruction and experience with hot glassworking. By the 1960s, there was a furnace in the basement of the college. The department continued to expand and moved to a new building with a larger, improved furnace.

Lawrie, Monro Turner's student turned assistant, completed her dream in the 1980s, when the stained glass section merged with the architectural glass section during his tenure as head of department. Born in Edinburgh in 1928, Lawrie left school with no qualifications and did various jobs before his National Service from 1947 to 1949. He then spent three years in the fire service before entering the ECA to study glass design and mural and life painting in 1951.

From 1956 to 1961, he assisted Monro Turner in establishing her Juniper Green workshop, which included building a furnace, and with some of her larger architectural commissions. In 1964, Lawrie designed and executed a window for the Loretto School chapel extension in Musselburgh. This was a windowed gable with blocks of coloured glass set in concrete.

Education was a major part of Lawrie's life too. He taught part-time in the School of Occupational Therapy at Astley Ainslie Hospital from 1961 to 1966, and in 1966, he rejoined the staff of ECA to teach in the mural and glass departments. In 1970, he succeeded Monro Turner on her retirement as head of the Department of Glass Design. He retired in 1989 and was succeeded by Ray Flavell.

Among the first commercial companies to benefit from graduates of the department was Caithness Glass. The company established in 1960 by the Hon. Robin Sinclair (later Lord Thurso) was at Wick in the extreme northeast of Scotland, where the traditional industries were fishing and farming. It was an area of high unemployment and there were few opportunities for young people. The company's goals were social, commercial and artistic. It was thought that the company would provide glass for the Atomic Energy Authority's new plant at Dounreay, but there is no evidence that this ever happened.

Domhnall O'Broin, an Irish graduate of ECA who had travelled widely throughout Europe visiting glassworks, particularly in Scandinavia, was responsible for the factory design and the planning of the project. Initially, the glassmakers were from Austria and Italy but the intention was always to train local people. In 1963, Paul Ysart joined the company as training officer and set up a full programme of training, which operated throughout the company's independent existence.

Conversation Piece by John Lawrie: glass forms that can be grouped in various ways and inspired by Walt Disney's Fantasia.

Courtesy Brian Blench

The Caithness Glass factory, Harrowhill, Wick, in about 1979.
Courtesy Brian Blench

The early Caithness production, with relatively unskilled workers, relied on the quality of the glass, which used the high-quality silica sand from Loch Aline, and relatively simple designs. These, unsurprisingly, showed considerable Scandinavian influence: basic functional shapes in clear crystal with, in some ranges, added colour inspired by the local landscape. The colours, peat, heather, moss green and twilight blue, remained in production for 20 years. Christopher Dresser would surely have approved.

Despite his burdensome role in the company, Paul Ysart's main interest remained in traditional paperweight making – millefiori canes and lampwork. In the seven years he was with the company, he worked on these in his spare time, often with the assistance of the young Peter Holmes. He made over 20 patterns with his "PY" signature cane and marketed them exclusively in the USA through the dealer Paul Jokelson. He retired from Caithness in 1970, and the following year set up his own studio at the Old Lighthouse, Harland, Wick, working with William (Willie) Manson Snr.

Five years later, he registered Paul Ysart Glass Ltd and purchased a furnace for £7,165.60. An "H" cane identified the standard paperweights, the "PY" cane being reserved for limited edition items. Paul Ysart changed the name of the company to Highland Paperweights Limited in 1977. He retired in 1979, and died in 1991 having made a significant contribution to glassmaking in Scotland for over 70 years.

A Canisbay decanter with Morven and Lybster tumblers, illustrating Domhnall O'Broin's legacy from his studies in Sweden. The names for the glass were all local places.

Copyright © Culture & Sport Glasgow (Museums)

Setting a new melting pot into the furnace at Caithness Glass. This was carried out at operating temperature.

Courtesy Scotland's Glass, copyright © Caithness Glass Co. Ltd

The next major development at Caithness was the establishment of an engraving department at the instigation of the chairman, George Mackie MP; however, someone was required to run this specialist operation. When Mackie asked Colin Terris if he would establish such a department, he said, "I don't want to prostitute your art." Terris replied, "I've been waiting for years for someone to take commercial advantage of me." He got the post.

Born in Kirkcaldy, Fife, in 1937, Terris was educated in Buckhaven and entered ECA in 1956, where he specialised in design, drawing, painting, glass and calligraphy. During his final year on the glass course, he spent some time at Foley College of Art in Stourbridge using its hot glass facilities and met some of the Caithness trainees doing the same thing. In 1960, Terris travelled to Norway on a scholarship to work with Alasdair Gordon, an earlier graduate of ECA, who was working as an engraver for Peter Kolderup at Hadeland. On his return, he took a teaching qualification at Moray House, and from 1961 to 1968 was an art teacher and lecturer in Fife.

On moving to Caithness in 1968, Terris assembled a team of engravers from ECA graduates, including Anne Robertson, David Gulland and Denis Mann. He also, of course, knew Paul Ysart and become fascinated by the technical quality and beauty of his paperweights. Writing some 25 years later, he said, "I was privileged to see him produce masterpieces as diverse as dahlias, dragonflies, cobras and ducks, and I was soon convinced that the paperweight was a natural form which could be adapted for a multitude of ideas other than traditional millefiori and lampwork designs.... Then – and even now – I was amazed that no one else had ever thought to try something other millefiori and lampwork."

With the assistance of Peter Holmes, Terris gained the knowledge and experience required to produce a new type of paperweight, and was soon able to plan the steps required to make this new form: abstract designs that could be viewed "from this angle or that, back lit or front lit as its location dictates." The first range was The Planets series produced in 1969. In later years, he also moved away from the traditional spherical shape to elongated, more monolithic shapes, though conservatism among collectors continued to demand "traditional" shapes.

The new techniques involved a new way of looking at what were, now, essentially decorative objects. The tools required for making them, apart from imagination, were as, Terris said, "simplicity itself: a spoon, a fork and a six-inch nail." By the company's 25th anniversary, over 1,000 different designs had been

Illusion, an abstract paperweight, Caithness Glass, 1979. One of over 1,000 paperweights that Colin Terris designed in the first 25 years of the company's existence, most of which were of the non-traditional type.

Courtesy Scotland's Glass, copyright © Caithness Glass Co. Ltd

produced, and the Caithness Paperweight Collectors' Society, formed by Terris in 1975, guaranteed a ready market for both the new abstract paperweights and the more traditional forms. Terris died in 2006, four years after his retirement from Caithness.

The new works at Wick proved attractive to visitors, and so in 1969 a small facility opened on the pier at Oban. This factory initially produced a range of paperweights in which coloured rods were trapped between layers of clear glass. In the same year, the company started making a range of jewellery using miniature millefiori paperweights. Ten years later, a new workshop and a visitor facility opened on the outskirts of Perth with a 25,000-ft^2 production area having four modern, gas-fired Thiesen furnaces.

Denis Mann, another ECA graduate, was an early recruit to the Caithness engraving team and soon became the departmental head. He, with Terris, designed the famous *Mastermind* trophy for the BBC. This was the first of many trophies for a wide variety of awards produced by the company, both engraved and in more-sculptural styles.

In the early 1980s, Mann began to experiment with a less traditional approach to engraving and started to explore kiln working. From 1992 to 1998, he worked part-time for Caithness, and in recent years he has continued to experiment with various glassmaking and decorating techniques in his studio in Wick. He is also deeply involved with North Lands Creative Glass.

North Lands Creative Glass is designated Scotland's Centre of Excellence in Glass Making and aims to stimulate interest in the possibilities of glass as an art form. In Lybster, a small fishing village on the north east coast, the centre enables glass artists, painters, sculptors, architects and designers to explore the technical and artistic potential of glass on its own or combined with other materials through summer master classes, an annual conference and residencies.

Top: Tim Shaw from Australia, artist in residence, 2007.

Bottom: Sky, Sea, Earth by Loretta Lowman, USA, artist in residence 2003

Copyright © North Lands Creative Glass

The BBC's Mastermind *trophy, designed by Colin Terris and Denis Mann and engraved by Mann.*

Copyright © Denis Mann

The decline in the market for high-quality ceramics and glass during the last decade of the 20th century led to the takeover of Caithness by Royal Worcester and Spode in 2001. Three years later, the situation had hardly improved, and Caithness Glass would have closed completely if Edinburgh Crystal had not bought the company, which now included Selkirk Glass (the studio formed by Peter Holmes and Ron Hutchison in 1977), in 2004, although the Wick factory was shut. Trading conditions have improved little since, and Caithness Glass went into administration in 2006. The company continues to produce paperweights from a new studio in Crieff as part of Dartington Crystal (Torrington) Ltd, an iconic English glassmaker.

Caithness's famous innovative abstract paperweights did not mean that the traditional types became obsolete in Scotland. The style of paperweights that Paul Ysart had made in Perth continued being made at Strathearn.

In 1968, Strathearn's first manager, Drysdale, left the company intent on establishing his own paperweight making business, Perthshire Paperweights. The company started in a disused school in Crieff, which proved unsuitable, so new premises had to be found. Financed with £7000, a new factory was built on a site opposite Strathearn. Production was of the traditional type of paperweight: millefiori and lampwork.

The original workforce consisted of John Deacons, Jack Allen from Vasart and Roy MacDonald and Peter McDougall, two apprentices from Strathearn. The factory ran on a profit-sharing basis with no designer. The staff worked out the patterns. There were standard production runs and five or six special limited editions each year. Anton Moravec was brought from Germany to be factory manager. The company's sales were worldwide, and, partly because of the low output, its paperweights were eagerly sought after, particularly after the factory closed in 2002.

In 1977, Holmes and Hutchison, both former employees of Caithness Glass, established Selkirk Glass at Linglie Mill, Selkirk. Holmes had served his apprenticeship under Paul Ysart but Selkirk's main production was non-traditional paperweights. Later, lampwork and sulphide paperweights were added as well as a range of animal sculptures and perfume bottles with gold or silver fused to the glass. Selkirk Glass was taken over by Edinburgh Crystal in 2004 and went into administration shortly after its new parent in 2006.

Four typical paperweight designs produced by Perthshire Paperweights. The company did not venture into the field of abstract designs.

Paperweights by Selkirk Glass. From top: Winter Dream, Nebula; Icepool. The company produced both abstract and traditional paperweights.

John Airlie at his furnace at Kirkhill Glass in 1972.
Courtesy Shiona Airlie

Meanwhile, John Airlie, who had entered the college as one of its oldest students at the age of 39 expecting to study sculpture, was drawn to the glass department. He became firm friends with Ken Wainwright, the department's technical wizard. The pair apparently spent many hours nursing the department's glass furnace. Airlie decided that the subject for his thesis would be to design a small experimental tank furnace to produce glass from the raw materials. The criteria were strict. It was to be inexpensive to build and operate, quiet and cool to work at, reliable and economical. It was to work without electrical power and to be suitable for a craftsperson or a student.

Paperweights were not the only area of Scottish glassmaking influenced by the ECA. The purpose of the Department of Glass Design was not to train people to work in large industrial units, rather to encourage smaller enterprises. Glass engravers need relatively little space in which to work. The glass comes to them ready made and only a lathe and a set of grinding and cutting wheels are required. However, hot-glass workers need hot metal from which to create, and this was not practicable in quantities small enough for a solo worker until the early 1960s.

Two Americans, Harvey Littleton and Dominick Labino, questioned whether it was possible to develop a small furnace suitable for an individual craftsperson. They held various symposiums and, with advice from an industrial glassblower, succeeded in developing a simple small furnace that could melt glass marbles or cullet. Thus, the studio glass movement was born.

When in Edinburgh, Lawrie built a similar small furnace at Monro Turner's studio at Juniper Green and one at the college, the studio glass movement had arrived in Scotland. One of the first artists to adopt the idea was Peter Layton, who set up a glass studio at his pottery in Morar in 1970, but he moved to London soon afterwards, where he continues to work in glass; perhaps the location was too remote.

Titania engraved by Norman Orr on cast glass with a wooden base designed and made by John Airlie. This was commissioned in 1972 as a house drama trophy for George Watson's College, Edinburgh.
Photograph Stuart MacLaren; copyright © George Watson's College.

Airlie was successful with his project, and, during his graduation year, he set up a propane-gas-fired furnace based on his thesis and established Kirkhill Glass. Here, he produced small soda-glass items. Meanwhile, he studied for a teaching qualification at Moray House, and in 1972 began teaching at Broughton High School in Edinburgh. Glass from Kirkhill is notable for its sparkling blue colour, a by-product of the kiln design. Unfortunately, Airlie had to close the studio in 1976 owing to ill health. Airlie had experimented with cast glass for engraving while at college and diversified into carved glass after graduation. Some of this glass remained free-form sculptures, but other pieces were used by Scottish engravers, notably two other students from the ECA: Norman Orr and Alison Kinnaird.

The Lindean Mill studio was established in 1977 near Galashiels by David Kaplan and Darryle Hinz. Kaplan is an American who studied in the glass departments of Goddard College, Vermont, USA, and ECA, and spent four years at various Swedish glasshouses, including Orrefors. The following year, Hinz moved on to set up a studio on Bornholm Island, Denmark. Kaplan was joined in 1978 by Annica Sandström, who had studied glass and ceramics in Sweden.

The early Lindean production was of glasses and other tableware often using both coloured and clear glass. In the early 1990s, the pair successfully developed a technique for making clear glass with a fused layer of colour-cased crystal. They also introduced the "graal" technique, which Orrefors developed in Sweden. Graal glass involves engraving, cutting or sandblasting designs on a gather of cold metal, covering it in clear glass, then reheating the whole piece and blowing it to the final desired shape; the result is a dramatic, though controlled distortion of the design. Lindean Mill successfully operates under the auspices of Kaplan and Sandström over 30 years later.

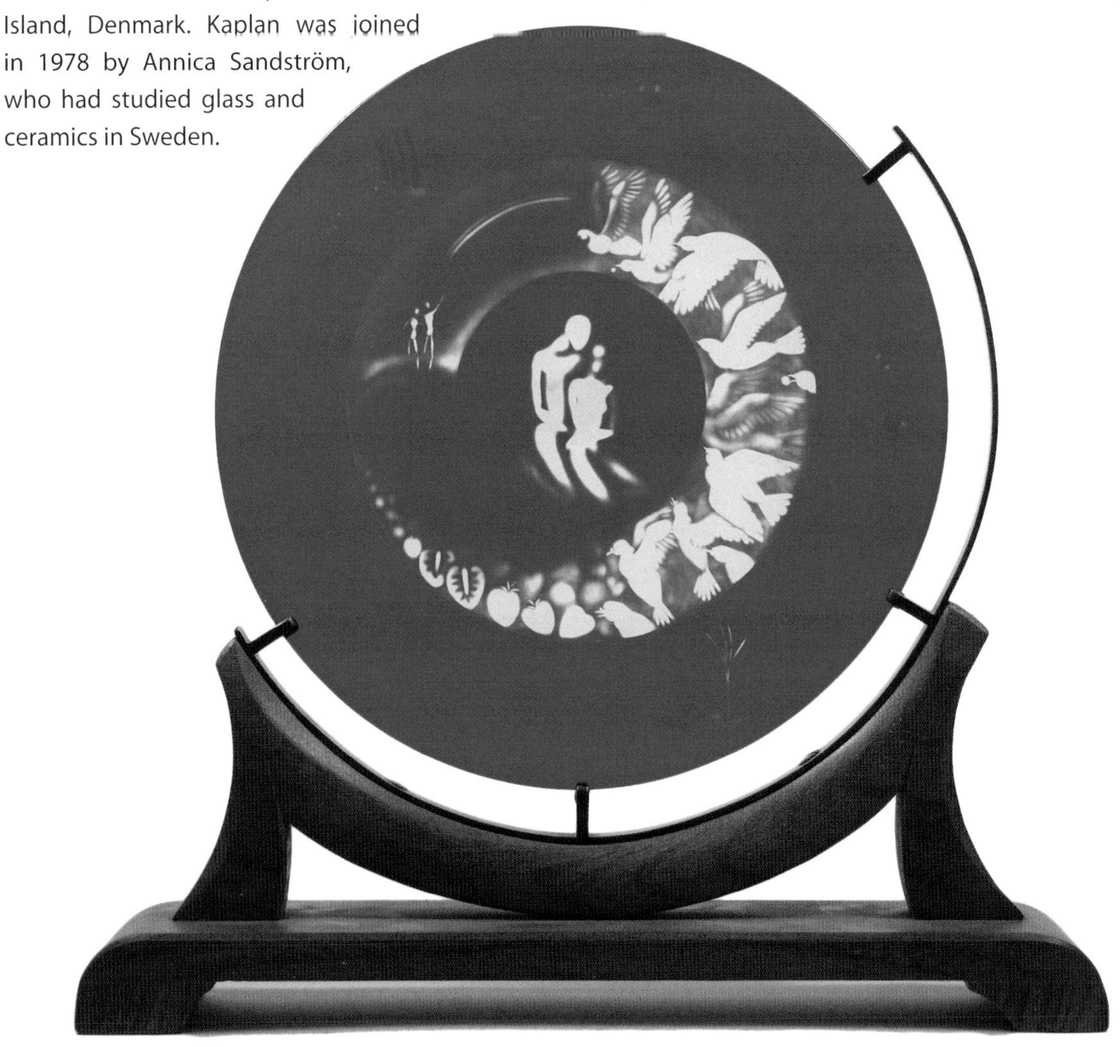

Colour-cased crystal made at Lindean Mill for engraving by Alison Kinnaird: "She is summer in the cold time between Christmas and Easter." This is another example of the frequent cooperation among modern glassworkers.

Throughout the centuries, glassmakers have been notoriously itinerant, despite the fact that their employers have always feared that they would give away trade secrets. The enclave of glassmaking on Murano was established not only because of the danger of fire if the glassmakers worked in Venice itself but also to try to prevent their moving to other areas. The Venetian glassmakers' secrets have long been prized throughout the world.

One such Venetian glass fan and itinerant glassmaker is Mike Hunter. Born in King's Lynn, Norfolk, in 1958, he began his apprenticeship at Wedgwood Glass at the age of 17: attaining the position of master glassblower 11 years later. Hunter became fascinated with Venetian glassware, particularly the intricate stemware, and, determined to find out how it was made, devoted seven years of his life to its study. In 1986, he moved to Welsh Royal Crystal as a stem maker. In 1989, he moved to Perthshire Paperweights for a short time before joining Lindean Mill in 1994 as production master for stemware. During this time, he had completed his *Manuscript on Glassmaking Techniques*.

In 1998, he established Twists Studio Glass in Selkirk to make contemporary glass based on the shapes and decoration of 16th and 17th century Venice and 18th century England. Since then, the studio has also branched out into other areas of art glass based on traditional techniques.

Alastair MacIntosh is another such itinerant with a love for Venetian techniques. Born in Falkirk, Stirlingshire, in 1951, he studied at ECA for four years before joining the department as a glass design technician for two years. He then moved to Paisley College of Technology where he undertook a two-year research project on high-purity luminescent glass.

He established MacIntosh Glass in Falkirk in 1981 to make air-twist wine glasses, perfume bottles, paperweights, vases and bowls. In 1987, MacIntosh joined the design team at Caithness Glass in Perth where, working closely with the company's senior glassmaker, Franco Toffolo, he made a major contribution to the range of paperweights with designs often inspired by his love of climbing, as well as to trophies and awards for sport and business.

Swirly by Mike Hunter. Made using the Italian roll-up technique and incorporating murrines and cane-worked swirls, this is typical of Hunter's modern interpretation of ancient Venetian techniques.

Helix scent bottle with black iridescent lustre by Alastair MacIntosh, 1982.

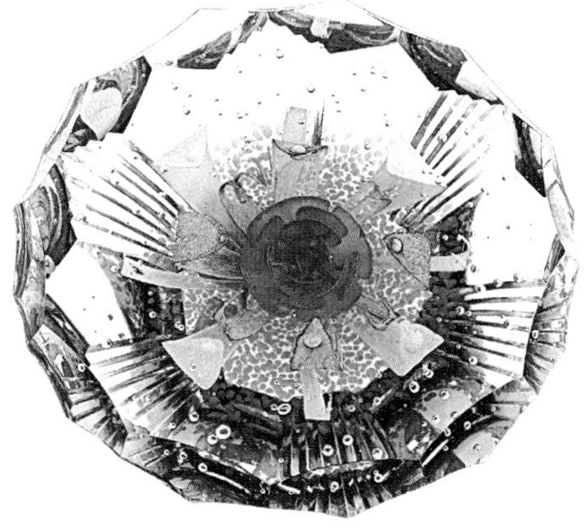

The Queen's Golden Jubilee paperweight was a limited edition, numbering just 30.

Designed by Colin Terris, made by Franco Toffolo, cut, engraved and polished by Martin Murray.

Glassmakers in Scotland do not simply concentrate on the more traditional methods. Joan Holdsworth was born in Blackburn, Lancashire, in 1948 and became attracted to glass while studying as a mature student at the nearby Accrington and Rossendale College. Holdsworth then studied at the ECA, where she won the Scottish Glass Society prize in 1996, her graduation year. The same year she set up a studio in Braga, Orkney.

Holdsworth takes her inspiration from the landscape around her and captures natural forms, patterns and textures using a variety of techniques. She often takes plaster casts of rocks, stones and sand patterns, which she uses to shape her glass in a kiln. Her techniques include layering and fusing sheet glass, pate de verre, slumping and casting. The results, often unpredictable and surprising, nevertheless reflect, though do not mirror, the accidents that occur in nature. In recent years, Holdsworth has been closely involved with North Lands Creative Glass.

The link between Scottish glass and that made in Newcastle upon Tyne, which originated in the 17th century, continues to this day, notably in the work of Jane Charles. Originally trained at North Staffordshire Polytechnic, Stoke on Trent, before studying traditional glass skills at Dudley near Stourbridge, she moved to Edinburgh in 1987 to set up her studio, Jane Charles Studio Glass. However, she travelled to Newcastle every month to make her glass, as she only had cold working equipment in Edinburgh.

Highly coloured bowls and vases are typical of Charles' production. Cutting and polishing add texture to her free-blown forms, and she excels in understanding the sculptural freedom only found in glass. Charles left Scotland in 1993 to make a permanent base in Newcastle, but the influence her glass has had on other glassworkers in Scotland is still felt.

Scotland seems to attract female glassmakers, among them Deborah Fladgate, who was born in Nicosia, Cyprus, and studied at the West Surrey College of Art and Design. She graduated in ceramics in 1979, and that year took part in her first glass exhibition. She then worked at Cowdy Glass, Newent, Gloucestershire, and with Antony Stern in London, before moving to the Royal College of Art to take a master of art degree in glass and set up a studio in Farnham, Surrey. Fladgate has held various visiting lectureships, and was artist in residence at Wedgwood Glass, King's Lynn, and at Dartington Crystal, Torrington, before relocating her studio to Scotland in 1990.

After 30 years working with glass, Fladgate is now based in Gateside, Fife. Her glassware is elegant and classical, often using coloured metal. She revels in the exploration of the various forms and the uses to which it can be put. Her "work is about the simplicities and complexities of glass and is an exploration of optical confusions. One's eye is drawn inside to discover what can only be glimpsed at first. The elements inside cannot ever be clearly or completely seen and are intangible and unexplained."

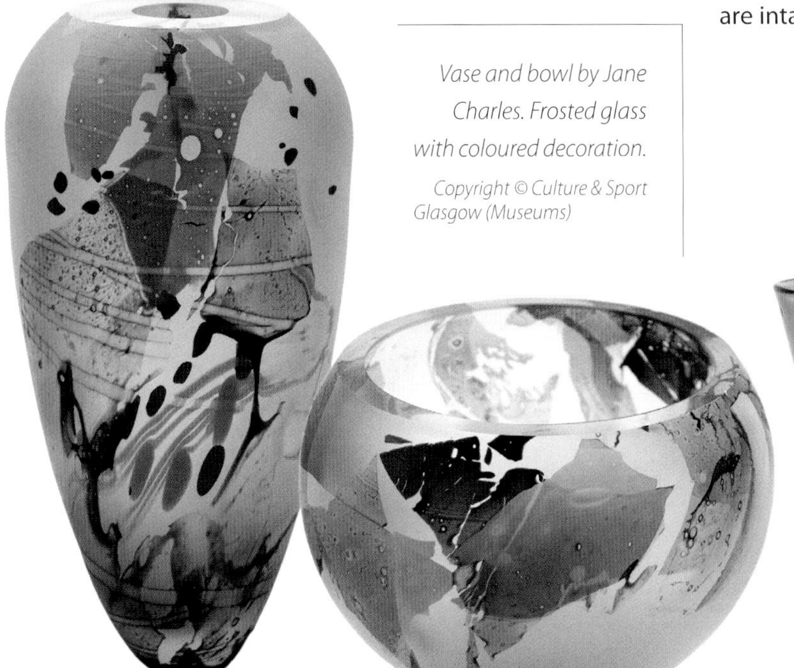

Vase and bowl by Jane Charles. Frosted glass with coloured decoration.

Clover cut bowl by Deborah Fladgate, 1994.

Zoë Gadsby's work is of a very different style. Born in Portsmouth, Hampshire, in 1973, Gadsby initially studied environmental art at Glasgow School of Art before moving on to a decorative glass course at Glasgow College of Building and Printing. She then worked on glass installations exploring light and colour before a further two years of study on architectural and kiln-formed glass. For over 10 years, Gadsby has used leaded and fused glass on various scales, often with geometric symbols, complex geometric patterning and vivid colours, to reflect naturally occurring chaotic forms combined with high-tech circuitry, and micro-photography of viruses, cells and even atoms.

Slumped and fused work by Zoë Gadsby.
Above: Hot White

Below: Big Red Multi Shimmer.

Bottom: detail from Red Flow.

Like Monro Turner, Anita Pate, a native Scot and an ECA graduate, won an Andrew Grant Travelling Scholarship, which she used to visit Venice, Murano and Athens. On her return, she established the Hourglass Studio in Edinburgh with Jenny Stevenson, where they reworked earlier glassmaking techniques. In 1978, Pate was an artist in residence at Sunderland Polytechnic before travelling to Australia and New Zealand where she worked in studio workshops and as head of the glass department at the Chisholm Institute in Melbourne, Australia. She returned to Scotland to establish her own studio at East Linton, East Lothian, where she specialised in sandblasting blown coloured glass. Since 1987, she has worked more in the field of large architectural glass, religious and secular, both sandblasted and stained, rather than smaller glass objects.

The Pilgrim Chapel, Stafford District General Hospital, showing the Vestry light – the pilgrim's scallop shell, by Anita Pate

Alison McConachie's deceptively simple forms involve detailed research, constant experimentation and a demand for perfection that result in objects of strange and compelling beauty. She worked originally on clear and sandblasted glass, often with applied trails of glass until a visit to Venice. There, she became enthralled with the richness of the city, the light on the water, the antiquity, the beauty and the elegance. This experience eventually resulted in her Ausonian series of bowls in which a clear gather of glass has rings of colour applied and the resulting "egg" is covered several times with clear glass. The whole is then reheated and blown to the required size. The result is sandblasted. Then a hide glue is applied; this contracts when gently heated and curls away from the surface taking a layer of glass with it. Her work is constantly "in process;" nothing is ever perfect; to her this is the challenge and joy of studio glasswork.

McConachie was born in Edinburgh in 1953, and studied at ECA from 1971 to 1975, before taking a master of art degree at the Royal College of Art, London. She than spent a year as studio assistant to Willem Heesen at De Oude Horn Glass Studio, Leerdam, the Netherlands, and a further year at Dent Glass in Cumbria. McConachie then returned to teach at the ECA, where she succeeded Flavell as only the fourth departmental head of glass in its 60-year history.

Bowl with sandblasted decoration by Alison McConachie.

Copyright © Culture & Sport Glasgow (Museums)

One development in recent Scottish glassmaking relatively unconnected with the ECA has been the re-emergence of lampworking. This is a technique of making objects, usually small ones, without using a furnace to melt the metal. The craft has flourished in Lauscha, Germany, since the 17th century, when oil-fuelled lamps were used to heat the glass, in the making of ornaments for Christmas trees. In the 20th century, lampworking appeared as what was often as a sideline for technical glassworkers using borosilicate glass, the glass used most often in laboratories, and gas flames. To many people, it is the sort of glassmaking associated with seaside and fairground souvenirs, little animals, model houses and other knick-knacks, but it is also a relatively cheap and speedy process for producing attractive objects or works of art.

One of the first people to introduce the technique to Scotland was Frits Akerboom. From Amsterdam, the Netherlands, he studied at the technical college in Deventer and the University of Leiden before moving to Scotland in 1971 as scientific glassblower at the University of St Andrews. From 1971 to 1972, he undertook day-release studies at ECA. His lampwork and slumped glass have been exhibited widely throughout Scotland and in Germany and Austria.

Willendorff bottle in multicoloured borosilicate glass by Frits Akerboom, signed and dated March 1976.

Copyright © Culture & Sport Glasgow (Museums)

Another incomer to Scotland is Ed Iglehart (*right*). Born in Baltimore, USA, in 1941, Iglehart studied chemistry at the University of Florida and graduated in 1965. He began making glass full-time in 1969, moved to Scotland three years later and established a workshop at North Glen, Palnackie, soon afterwards.

Iglehart is a committed environmentalist and his working methods and the final products are intimately associated with the Earth. He has experimented with making glass from a variety of natural materials: a mixture of 85% Dalbeattie granite, 5% sea salt, 5% seashells and 5% borosilicate waste and a trace of local barite produced a dark green glass that worked well but proved difficult to anneal. He has also experimented with melted whisky bottles – a "natural" material in Scotland! One constant of his production is the lampworked mushroom form but to this he has added a wide range of decorative and functional items, including chandeliers from bottles. Using borosilicate glass, he has also produced dramatic architectural items, including a set of wind chimes engraved by David Gulland for presentation to the Prince of Wales on his marriage in 1981.

One glassmaker who definitely confirms the maxim that small is beautiful is Tom Young. He was born in Glasgow in 1938 and worked as a glassblower with R. & J. Wood before moving to be scientific glassblower at Loughborough University. In 1967, he became the chief scientific glassblower at Stirling University, where he remained until he established Village Glass in Bridge of Allan in 1979. In contrast to Iglehart, Young works solely with preformed glass rod and tubing to produce a wide range of practical and decorative wares.

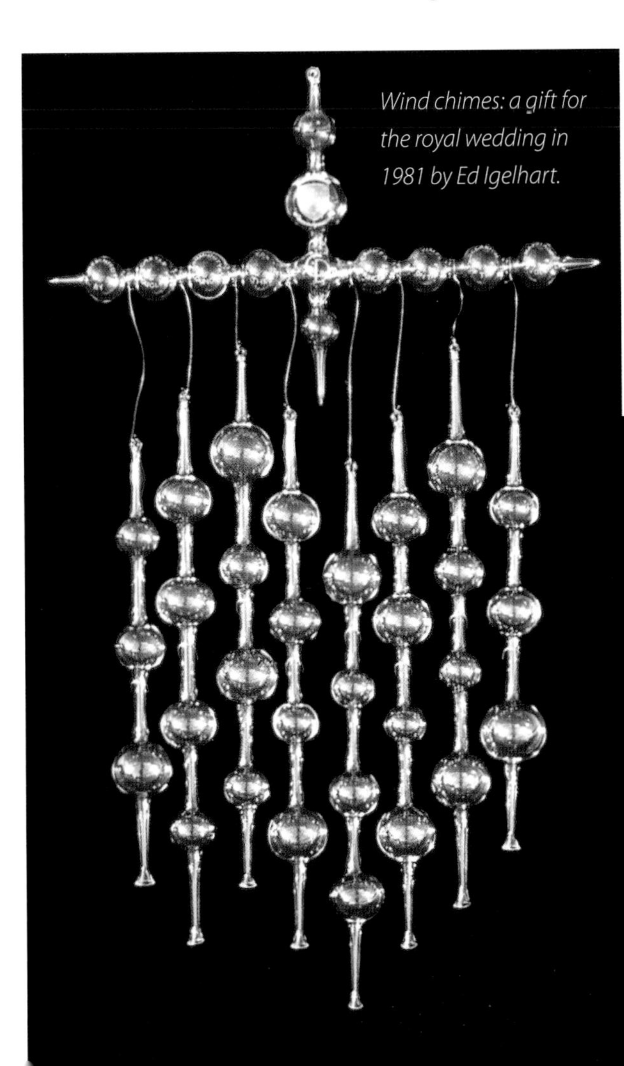
Wind chimes: a gift for the royal wedding in 1981 by Ed Igelhart.

Bon-bon dish, with glass sweets by Tom Young

All photographs on this page courtesy Brian Blench

Ian Pearson was born in Croydon, Greater London, in 1953 and worked as a scientific glassblower for various companies in England before moving to manage the scientific glass department at UKAEA, Dounreay, in 1981. During this period, he gave artistic demonstrations of lampworking to local schools and charities. In 2000, Pearson set up his own studio in Thurso, where he has an individual, even idiosyncratic, approach to his creations. They are always carefully planned, displaying both wit and ingenuity. In startling contrast to Dresser's theory, he feels that "it is up to all glass artists to demonstrate the success of craftsmanship over the natural wish of the material." But then that is what Dresser did in practice! Pearson still works at UKAEA, but as the record manager following the closure of the glassblowing department, while still undertaking glass commissions for Thurso Glass Studio.

It is perhaps fitting to end this brief survey of Scottish glassmaking in the 20th century with glass engraving. This was the craft that the authorities thought would be the mainstay of the department that they asked Monro Turner to found. They had not comprehended her breadth of vision or her willingness to broaden the range of instruction in the department.

One of Monro Turner's earliest students was Alison Geissler. Born Alison McDonald in Edinburgh in 1907, the same year as the ECA was founded, she had studied design at the college between 1925 and 1931. Here she met and married William Geissler, a lecturer in painting and anatomy. On her return to Edinburgh after the war, Geissler decided to re-establish her career as an artist. The then head of the design department, Herbert Henry, suggested glass engraving. She was at first unwilling, as she wanted to paint, but thought it impolite to ignore the advice, perhaps remembering that her maternal grandfather has been a glass engraver at the Edinburgh and Leith Flint Glassworks at Norton Park. Among her contemporaries in the fledgling department was Harold Gordon, who later set up a studio in Forres and taught Alison Kinnaird.

Post-war restrictions made life difficult for freelance artists, but Jenners, the Princes Street department store, agreed to sell Geissler's work on glasses it provided; however the quality of the glass was often unsuitable for engraving. Later, she found that Edinburgh Crystal was prepared to provide blanks to her design. In 1950, the Scottish Craft Centre

Top: Ian Pearson working on a thistle candleholder.

Right: Tilt by Ian Pearson. A fun, abstract sculpture in borosilicate glass, 43-cm tall.

Copyright © Duncan McLachlan, Studiograff, Caithness

Russian Dancer engraved on an Edinburgh Crystal blank by Alison Geissler.

Copyright © Culture & Sport Glasgow (Museums)

opened in Edinburgh, and her first exhibits there led to requests for specific items, and, from then on, she worked largely to commission. Such work usually involves a slavish adherence to the purchaser's wishes but she often included details or even whole concepts that revealed her impish sense of humour. Geissler received an MBE in 1991 for her services to the craft. At 102, she is currently (November 2009) the oldest living graduate of ECA.

Another mature student to study under Monro Turner was Norman Orr. He had just started an apprenticeship in the glass industry when he joined the Royal Marines by lying about his age at the outbreak of war in 1939. After the war, he joined Edinburgh Crystal designing patterns and learning to cut and engrave glass. In 1964, he left the company and took evening classes at ECA in glass engraving, drawing and painting. He soon became recognised as one of Europe's leading glass engravers. Working almost exclusively to private commission, Orr's favourite subjects were animals depicted with remarkable realism, something that also extended to his artwork, as he is also considered to be the leading artist for Scotland's wildlife. He died in 1993.

David Gulland entered the ECA in 1951 at the age of 17. After graduating, he spent 12 years teaching before joining Caithness Glass as a designer and engraver. In 1977, he set up his own decorating studio in Dumfries. Gulland's subject matter includes wildlife and plant forms, and also the design and use of calligraphy and heraldry, often on sculptured blocks that provide depth and internal reflections to offer simultaneous images. His commissions are often ecclesiastical, and include the porch doors and windows for his own church, St John's Scottish Episcopal Church.

It is not always true that friendship and successful business go hand in hand, but for Wilma Mackenzie and Marjorie Campbell it is. Mackenzie, born in Dunoon, Argyll, in 1960, joined Edinburgh Crystal in 1977 to serve an apprenticeship under Lonie. She left the company in 1986 to work as freelance copper-wheel engraver. At a 1987 meeting of the Scottish Glass Society, Mackenzie met Campbell, a graphic artist with an interest in glass designing. They became good friends, and in 1989, they formed a partnership, Luckenbooth Glass Engraving. Campbell designed the glass, which was often produced by Adrienne McStay, and Mackenzie engraved it. The partnership continued until Campbell's death in 1999. In 2004, Mackenzie established her own studio in Tarbert, Argyll. Working largely to commission, she has a wide range of subjects but is particularly interested in wildlife and flower subjects.

Fox engraved on an Edinburgh blank by Norman Orr.
Copyright © Max Kimber

Right: Detail from a drawing by Norman Orr.
Courtesy Shiona Airlie

Group of four glasses engraved by David Gulland with motifs to represent Scotland, Ireland, England and Wales.
Copyright © Culture & Sport Glasgow (Museums)

Without doubt, the most successful and influential Scottish engraver of the post-war era is Alison Kinnaird, MBE. Born in Edinburgh in 1949, she took a degree in Celtic studies and archaeology at Edinburgh University and studied at ECA in the Department of Glass Design, having already spent a year studying and learning engraving under Harold Gordon at his Forres studio. In 1971, she held her first solo exhibition and has since exhibited worldwide. Kinnaird has moved over the years from simple engraved pieces of crystal glass to working on high-quality crystal blocks made to her specification by renowned companies such as Corning Glass and on colour-cased crystal from Lindean Mill.

One of her main subjects is the human body, though her imagination seems boundless. She constantly reviews the opportunities provided by glass engraving, and in recent years has experimented with dichroic glass and engraved glass illuminated by LEDs.

One work in particular, Psalmsong (below), which was designed in 2003 for the Scottish Parliament building, illustrates the breadth of her imagination. This 3-m long work combines glass art with light and music for the Scottish harp. The melody *Psalmsong*, which is based on Gaelic psalms and was composed and performed by Kinnaird on harp, cello and the glass itself, was fed into a computer to sample the sound waves. These produced the interlacing Lissajous patterns that she engraved onto 24 crystal glass panels. The patterns combine with the human figure to represent the emotion of the music. Slips of dichroic glass under each panel, which have light transmitted though them using fibre optics, introduce colour to further suggest emotional states. An interesting shadow that appeared on the wall behind the panels when Kinnaird was playing with the lighting is printed on a linen banner. This now hangs behind the piece to give "it a new scale and a lot of dignity."

Over the course of its 400-year history, Scottish glass has come full circle. Hay founded an industry intent on producing glass for wealthy patrons. The rich and the favoured bought his windows and his wine glasses. Within two centuries, glass had become available to everyone, thanks to the technology of mass production. A world without glass is unthinkable today because of those developments.

Psalmsong by Alison Kinnaird. This spectacular work measures 3-m long by 40-cm tall by 1.5-cm. thick.

Copyright © Robin Morton

The industry Hay began became famous throughout the world. Scottish bottles were to be found in every part of the globe. Fleets of ships and hundreds of thousands of factories once depended on glass made in Scotland. But Scotland is no longer part of that mass production and the great glass factories have all but disappeared; like so many other Scottish industries, glassmaking is a victim of rising manufacturing costs and cheap labour elsewhere in the world.

In the 21st century, the glass made in Scotland has once more become a luxury commodity. Contemporary Scottish glass is an often an expensive indulgence produced by artists working in small studios to produce beautiful, high-quality objects. Hay's glassmakers knew many of the techniques they use, but the studio glass movement has pushed the technical and artistic boundaries further. Scottish glass is once more recognised for its quality and artistry rather than for its quantity. Their predecessors of the last 400 years would be proud of today's glassworkers, their innovation and the quality of their work, attributes they too had in abundance.

An example from Streetwise by Alison Kinnaird.

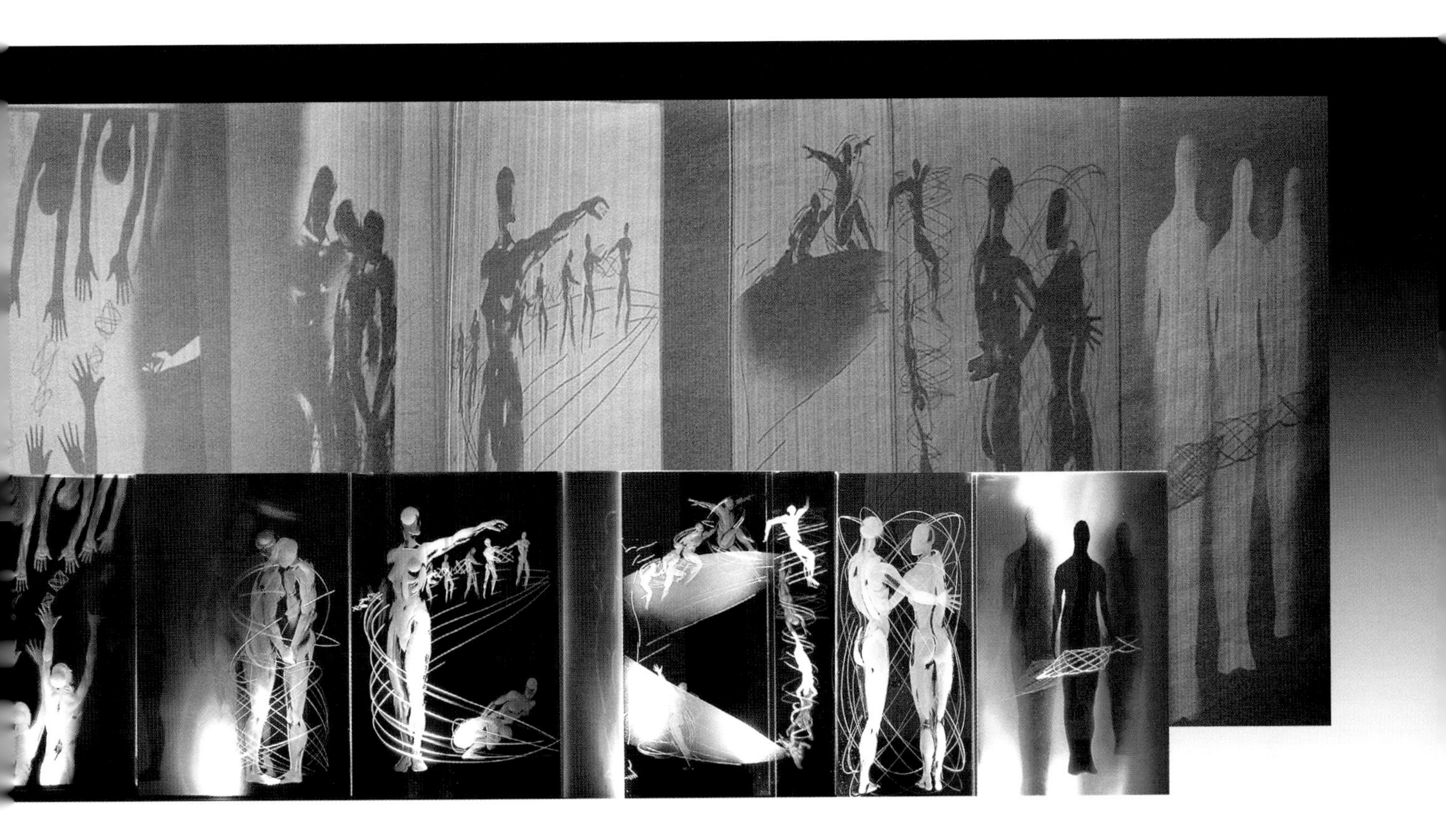

Showcase

Examples of Scottish Craftsmanship

Studio

From left: Perfume bottle in blue-cased glass by Anne Fleming; black glass cylinder with silver-leaf decoration, sandblasted and etched by Paul Woods; vase by Ed Iglehart, borosilicate glass with blue metal oxides; striped bottle by Anita Pate, c.1977; 1920s Monart cameo experiment by the Ysart family and Moncrieff chemist Jimmy Walker.

Left: Whaligoe, a cast glass sculpture by Marea Timoko, New Zealand, artist in residence at North Lands Creative Glass, 2005. It is inspired by the women who carried loads of herring from the sea, in creels, up 350 steps.

Below left: Clear bowl with coloured inclusions by Paul Musgrove.

Right: Opaque bowl with brown and white enamel and cane decoration by Jenny Antonio.

MONCRIEFF SCOTLAND
Monart Ware

Right: 35.5-cm tall Monart vase in green and black with gold aventurine inclusions, shape UA.

Arantes Collection

Below: Monart handled vase, white inner, ribbed grey and ochre stripes, shape I.

Courtesy Broadfield House Glass Museum

Soft bowl in blue glass by Deborah Fladgate, 1990.

Engraving

Left: Caithness vase engraved in Autumn Leaves pattern.

Right: Engraved Caithness decanter by Denis Mann. The engraving transforms the shape of the glass into a cartoonish, moustachioed bandsman, playing a trumpet.

Left: Strathearn goblet inscribed Pollok House, engraved by Alasdair Gordon.

Right: Detail of bison, engraved on a glass block by Harold Gordon, 1979.

Engraving

Engraved glasses, with the Snow Queen in background, by Wilma MacKenzie

Bowl hand-blown by Jane Charles and sandblasted by Julia Linstead inside and outside.

Photography Chael Merika, Washington Chase Collection

Paperweights

From top, then bottom row, right to left:

Green paperweight with oxide trails by Charles Ramsey, 1980.

Paul Ysart coloured sulphide of an Arab's head.

Courtesy Broadfield House Glass Museum

Willie Manson double hammerhead shark, 72 mm.*
John Deacons super magnum mushroom with garland, 2009, 100 mm.
Peter McDougall, unfaceted 3D flowers, 2009, 76 mm.

Perthshire millefiori paperweight, 1974.
Millefiori door knob mounted on brass fitting, Vasart Glass 1956 to 1964

Courtesy Glass Study Association, France

Acknowledgements

Without the support of museums and galleries across the UK, this book would never have been written. Our thanks go to Aberdeen Art Gallery & Museums; the Bennie Museum in Bathgate; Broadfield House Glass Museum, Kingswinford; Burghley House; the City of Edinburgh Museums and Galleries; Culture and Sport Glasgow; East Ayrshire Council; the National Library of Scotland; the National Museums of Scotland; Perth Museum; Science & Society Picture Library; Peter Stubbs (www.edinphoto.org); Paul Adair (Perth and Kinross Council); Denis Hebden; Max Kimber, David Fisher; Jim MacRae; and Robin Morton for helping us with photographs for this book.

We also owe a debt of gratitude to many individuals. Dr Anthony Lewis, Curator of Scottish History at Glasgow Museums, provided invaluable facts about 18th century documents and shared his research freely. Alison Brown, Curator of European Decorative Art from 1800 at Glasgow Museums, spent more hours than she ever imagined she would working with us in the glass stores, and her colleague, Celine Blair, made the process of photographing the collections there a real pleasure.

David Scarratt, Curator at the Museum of Edinburgh and at Lauriston Castle, took days from his schedule to share with us the marvellous collections and archives he looks after. Anne Geddes at East Ayrshire Council provided information about Kilmarnock, and Anne Thornton and her wonderful volunteers at the Bennie Museum made any visit there a real pleasure. Roger Dodsworth was generous with his time at Broadfield House Glass Museum.

Sandra Martin in Perth, Frank Little in Edinburgh, Kate Gillespie in Aberdeen and Lesley Castell at Museums and Galleries Scotland all smoothed our path and made our task so much easier. Dr John Cruikshank generously gave permission for us to draw on the Ford Ranken Collection in Edinburgh, and without Jill Turnbull's exhaustive research into early glass in Scotland and her generosity in sharing that knowledge with us, our book would have been all the poorer.

Adam Bergius refreshed memories, and Lindsay Arbuthnot provided information about her father, Angus Sillars. John Lawrie's memories of Helen Monro Turner and life at Edinburgh College of Art helped us greatly in writing the final chapter. Thanks, too to Nicola at pressedintime for her knowledge of pressed glass, and David Fisher for his anecdote from Canada.

Frank Andrews initiated this book, supported us at every stage and set up the Scotland's Glass website to promote the glass of this lovely country. He also provided numerous photographs. We are in his debt. Special thanks must also go to the best editor we have worked with, Christine Hudson. We would have been lost without her skill and patience. We must also thank our publisher, David Encill, who was brave enough to commit to this project and without whom we would have had very few illustrations indeed.

But last and certainly not least, an enormous thank you to all the glassmakers across the country who gave us support. We really could not have written this without you!

SHIONA AIRLIE
&
BRIAN J. R. BLENCH

Index